COLOR BY NUMBER

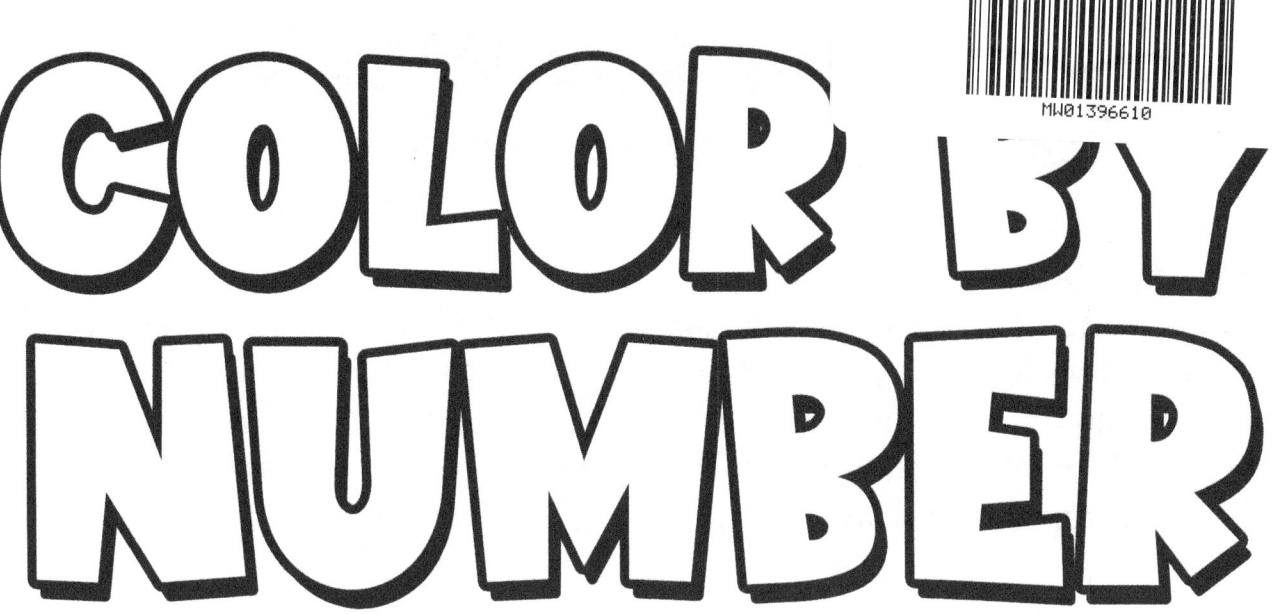

ALL RIGHTS RESERVED

No part of this publication may be reproduced, distributed, or transmitted in any form or by any means, including photocopying, recording, or other electronic or mechanical methods, without the prior written permission of the publisher, except in the case of brief quotations embodied in critical reviews and certain other non-commercial uses permitted by copyright law.

COLOR BY NUMBER
Coloring made fun and easy!

RELAX AND HAVE FUN
Let your worries slip away as you immerse yourself in coloring these beautiful images. Feel free to color while listening to your favorite music, watching TV, or simply lounging in bed - do whatever relaxes you the most! You can even take the coloring book with you anywhere you go, whether it's on the train or at a cafe. Coloring is therapeutic and an excellent way to relieve stress and promote relaxation.

CHOOSE YOUR COLORING TOOLS
Everyone has their preferred coloring tools, whether it's markers, crayons, colored pencils, or even paints! Don't hesitate to use whichever tool you like best. However, if you decide to use markers or paints, it's a good idea to place a blank sheet of paper or cardboard behind each image to prevent colors from bleeding onto the next page.

TEST OUT YOUR COLORS
Feel free to experiment with colors on our Color Chart located at the back of the book. You can utilize "Your Color Palette" to create your own unique color combinations, then cut this page out to compare each time you color. This way, you can ensure the colors match your preferences.

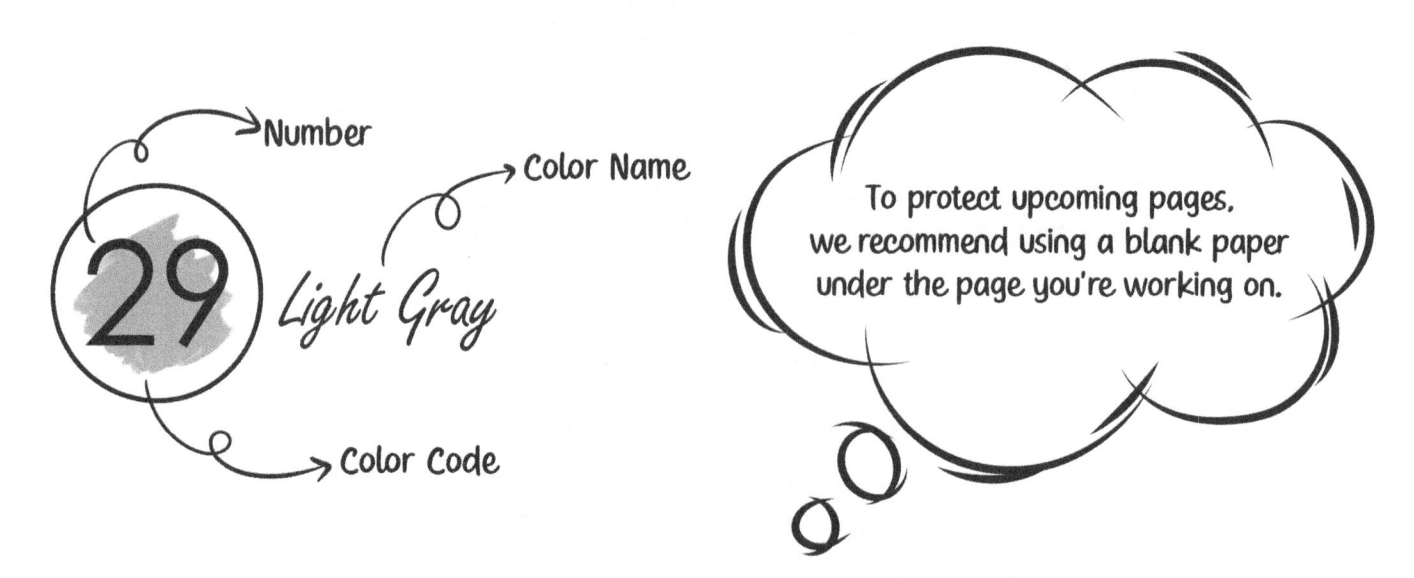

> Number → 29 ← Color Name: *Light Gray*
> Color Code

To protect upcoming pages, we recommend using a blank paper under the page you're working on.

Relax and Enjoy!

YOUR COLOR PALETTE

1 _____ 11 _____ 21 _____
2 _____ 12 _____ 22 _____
3 _____ 13 _____ 23 _____
4 _____ 14 _____ 24 _____
5 _____ 15 _____ 25 _____
6 _____ 16 _____ 26 _____
7 _____ 17 _____ 27 _____
8 _____ 18 _____ 28 _____
9 _____ 19 _____ 29 _____
10 _____ 20 _____ 30 _____

THIS BOOK BELONGS TO

....

....

....

....

....

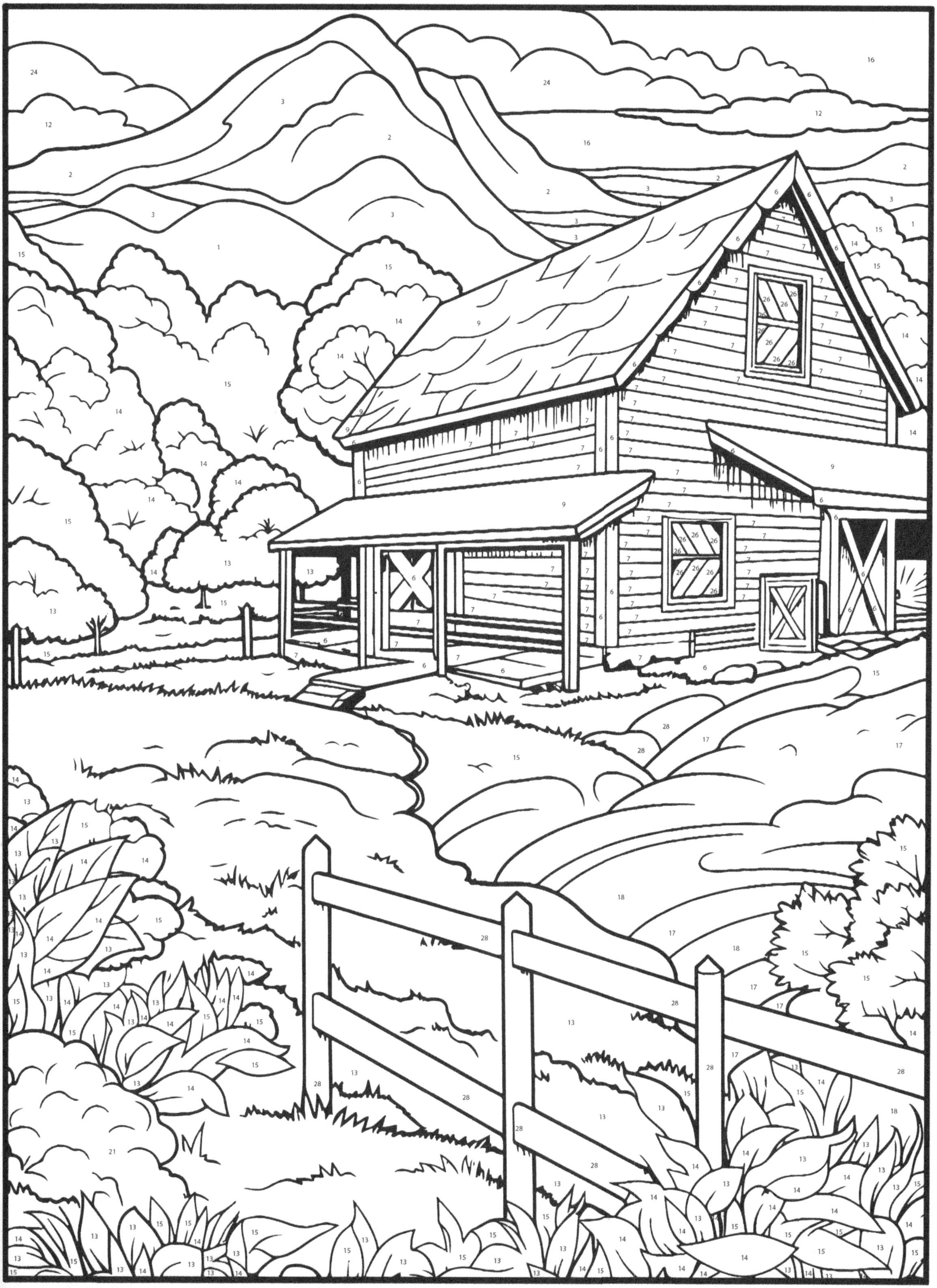

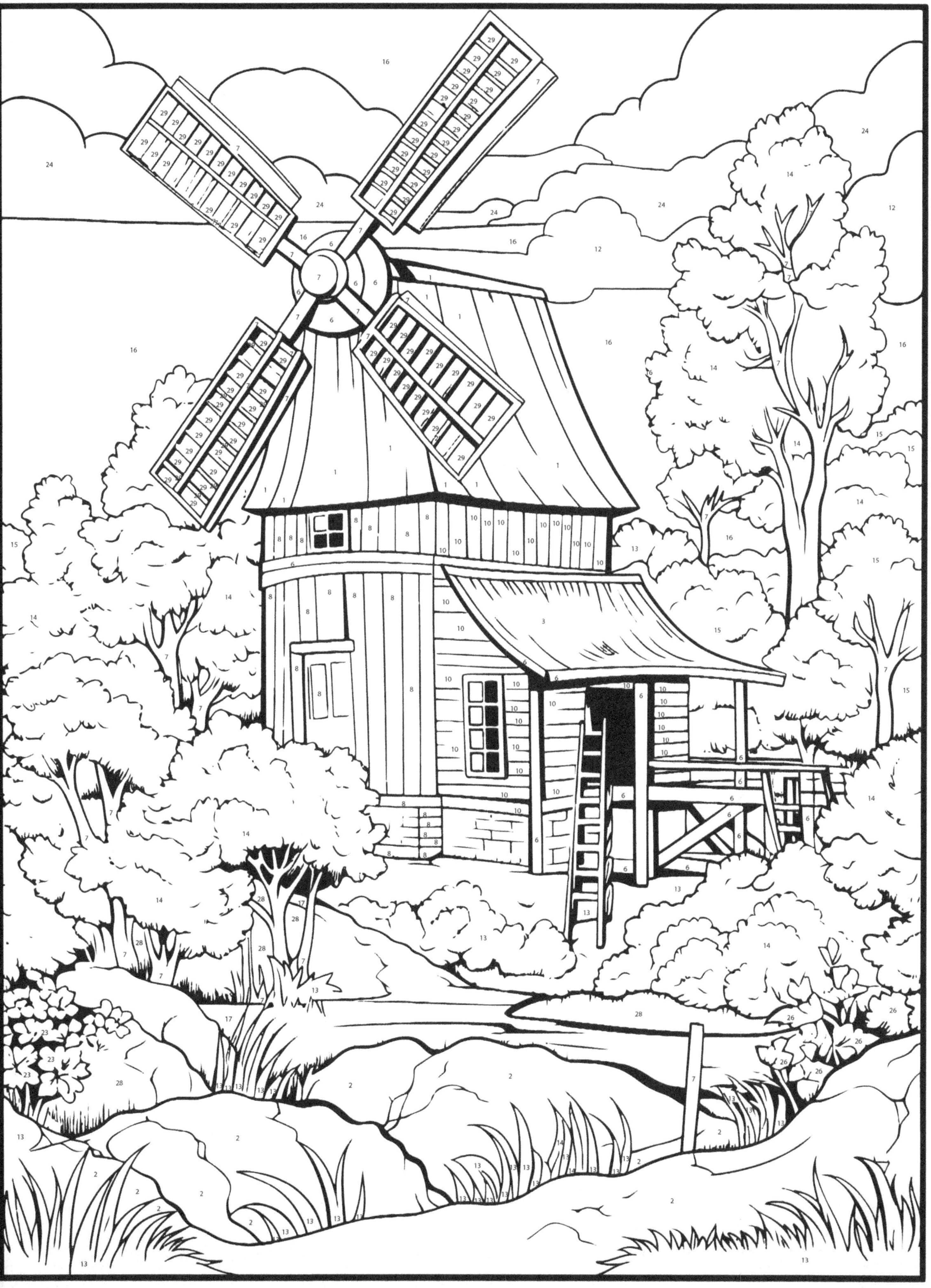

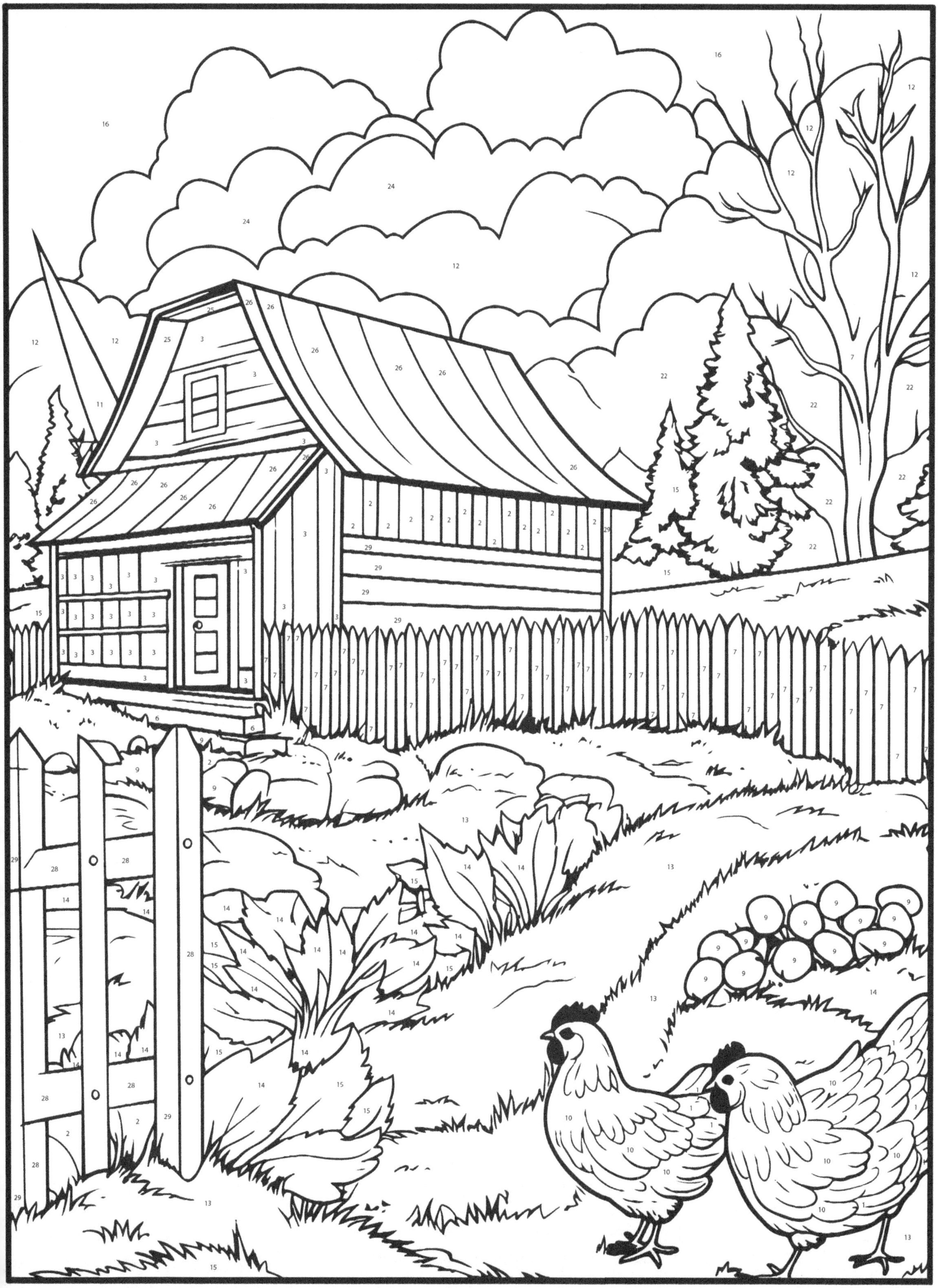

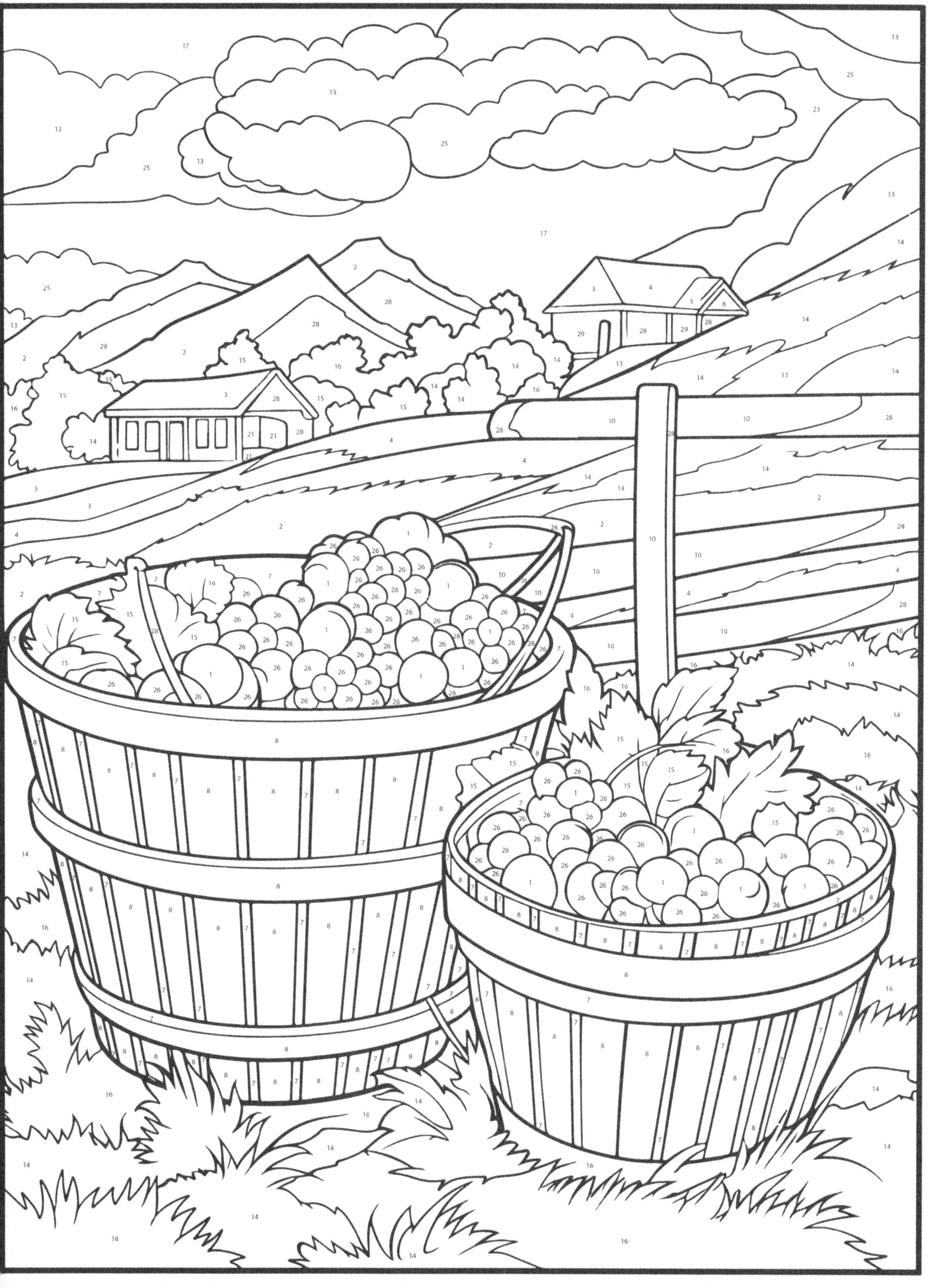

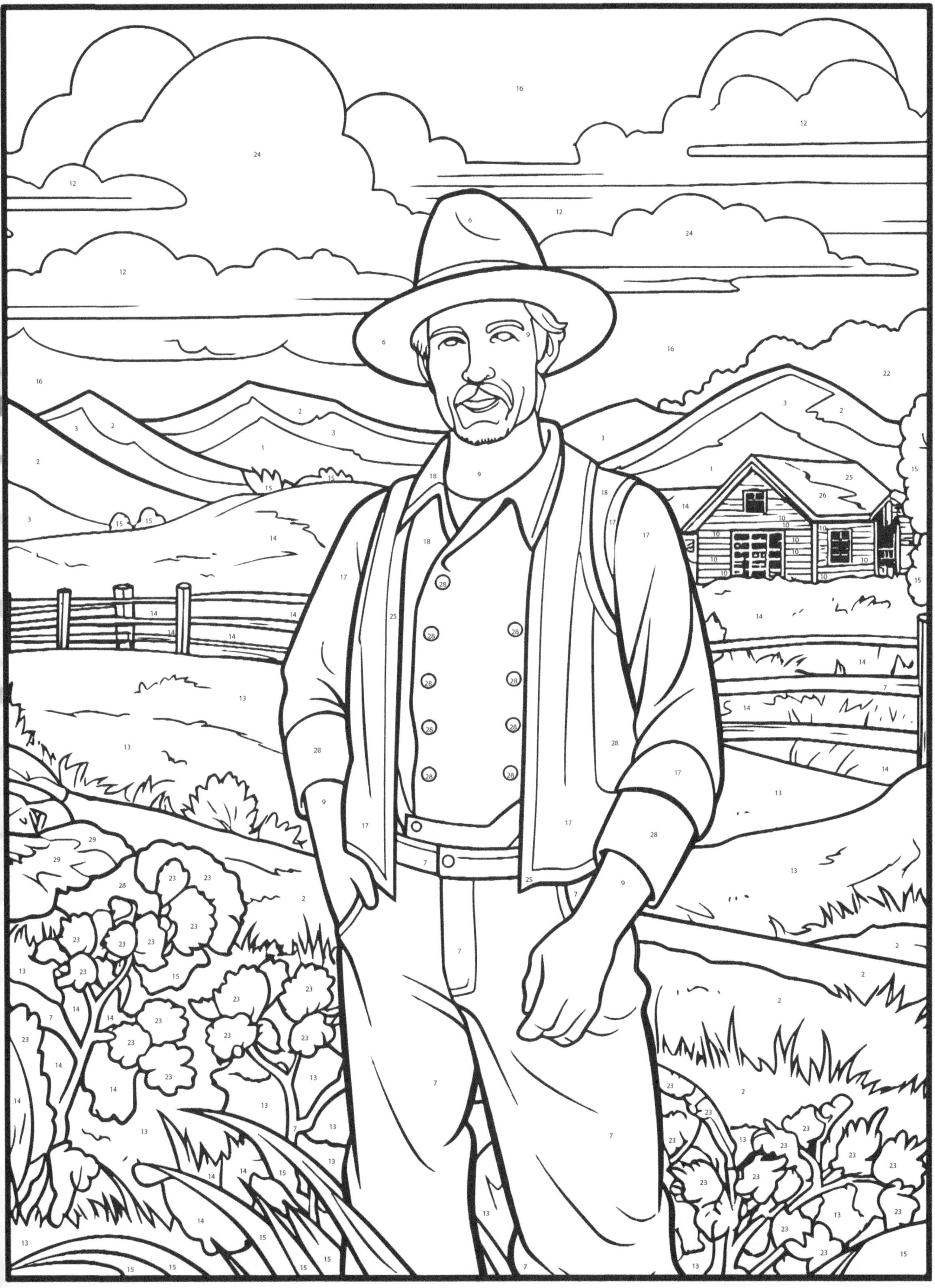

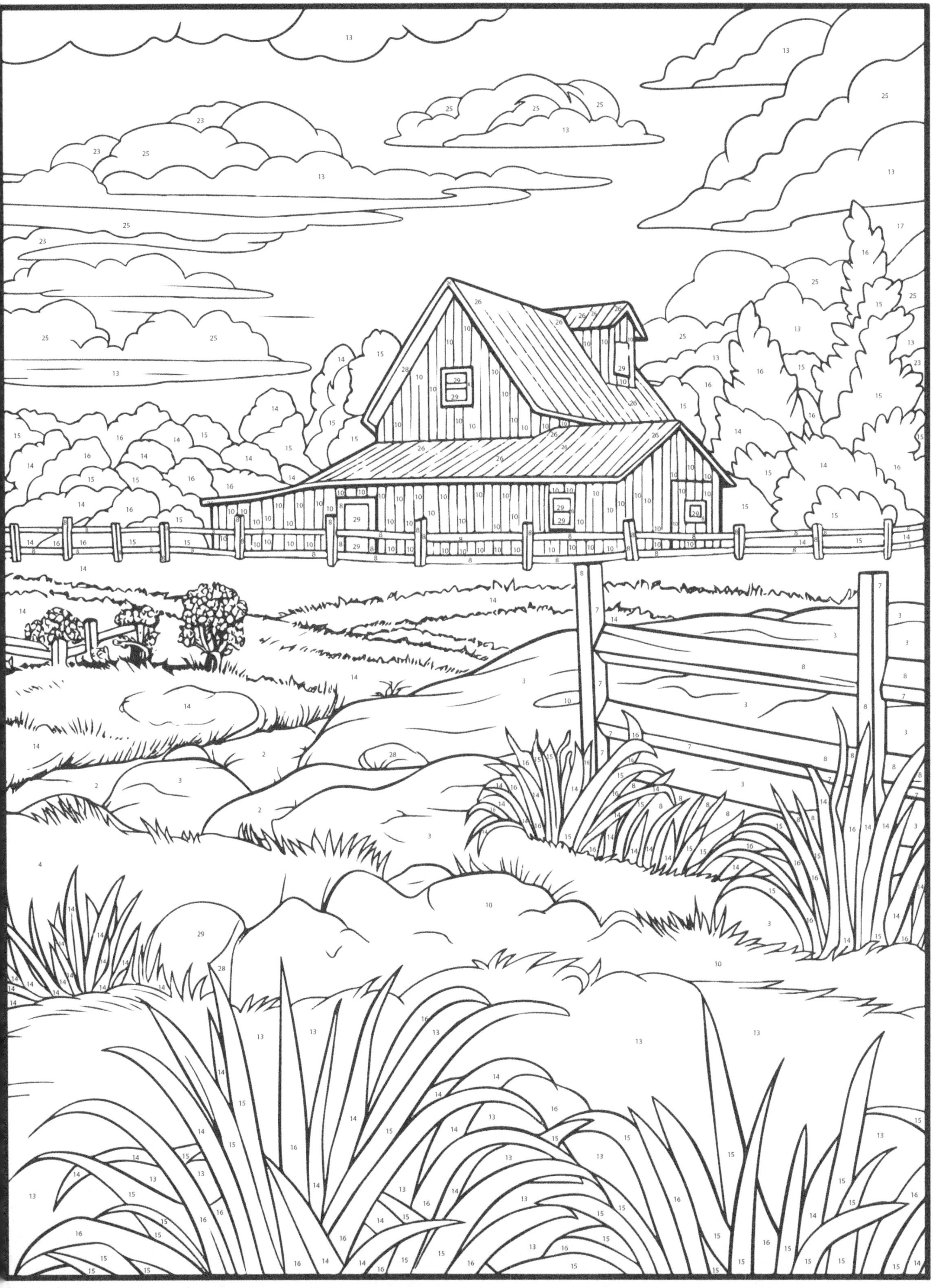

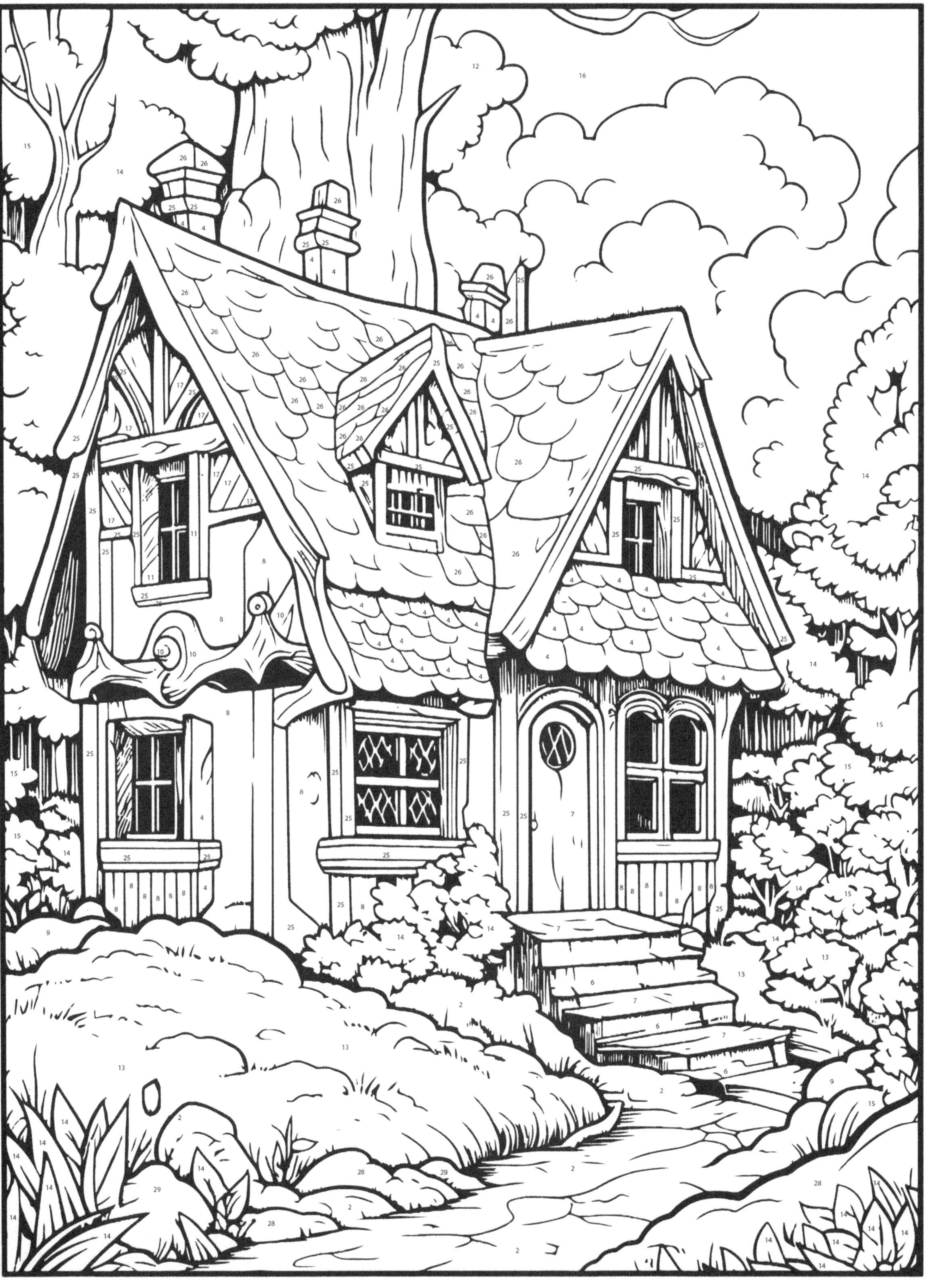

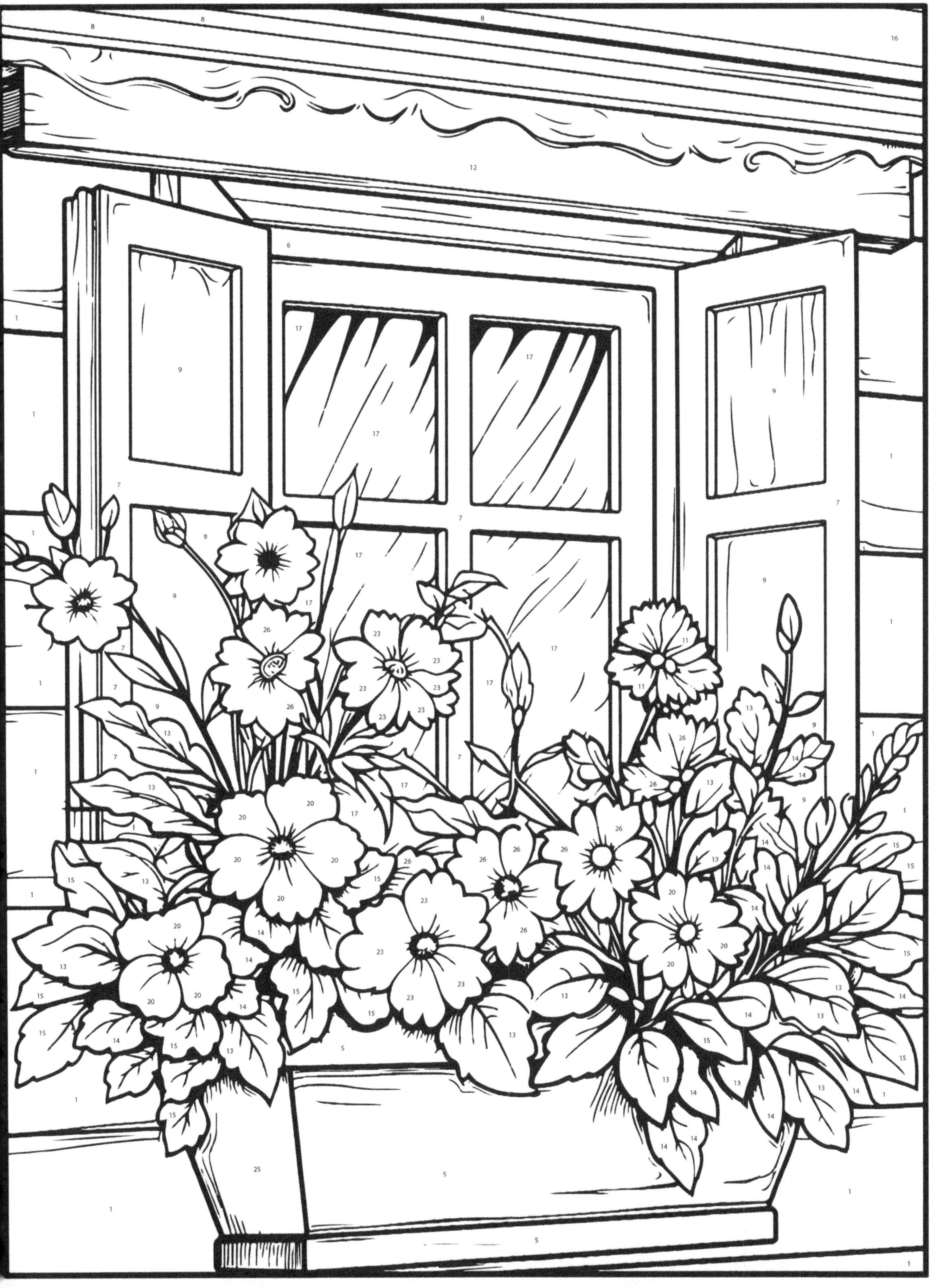

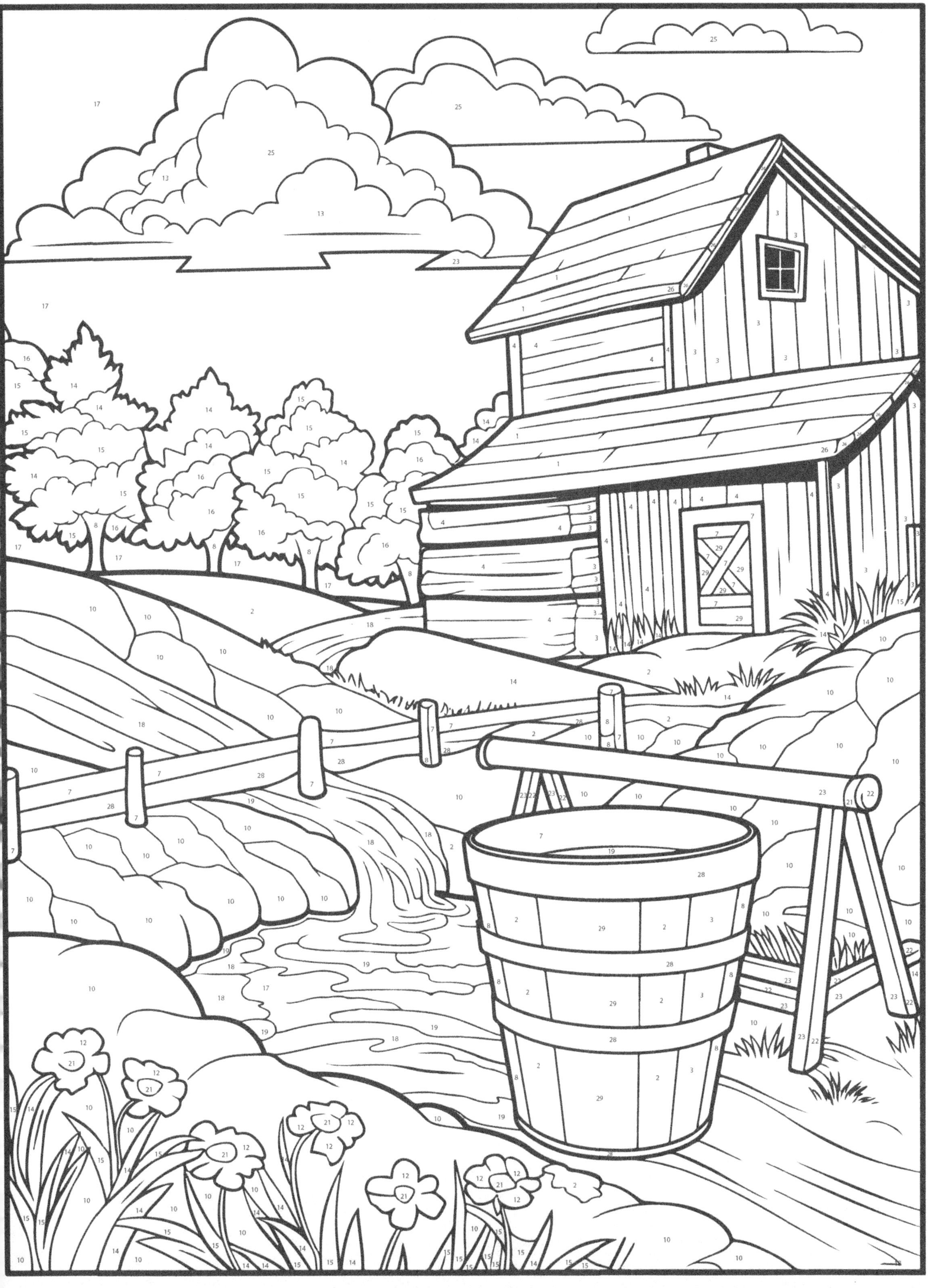

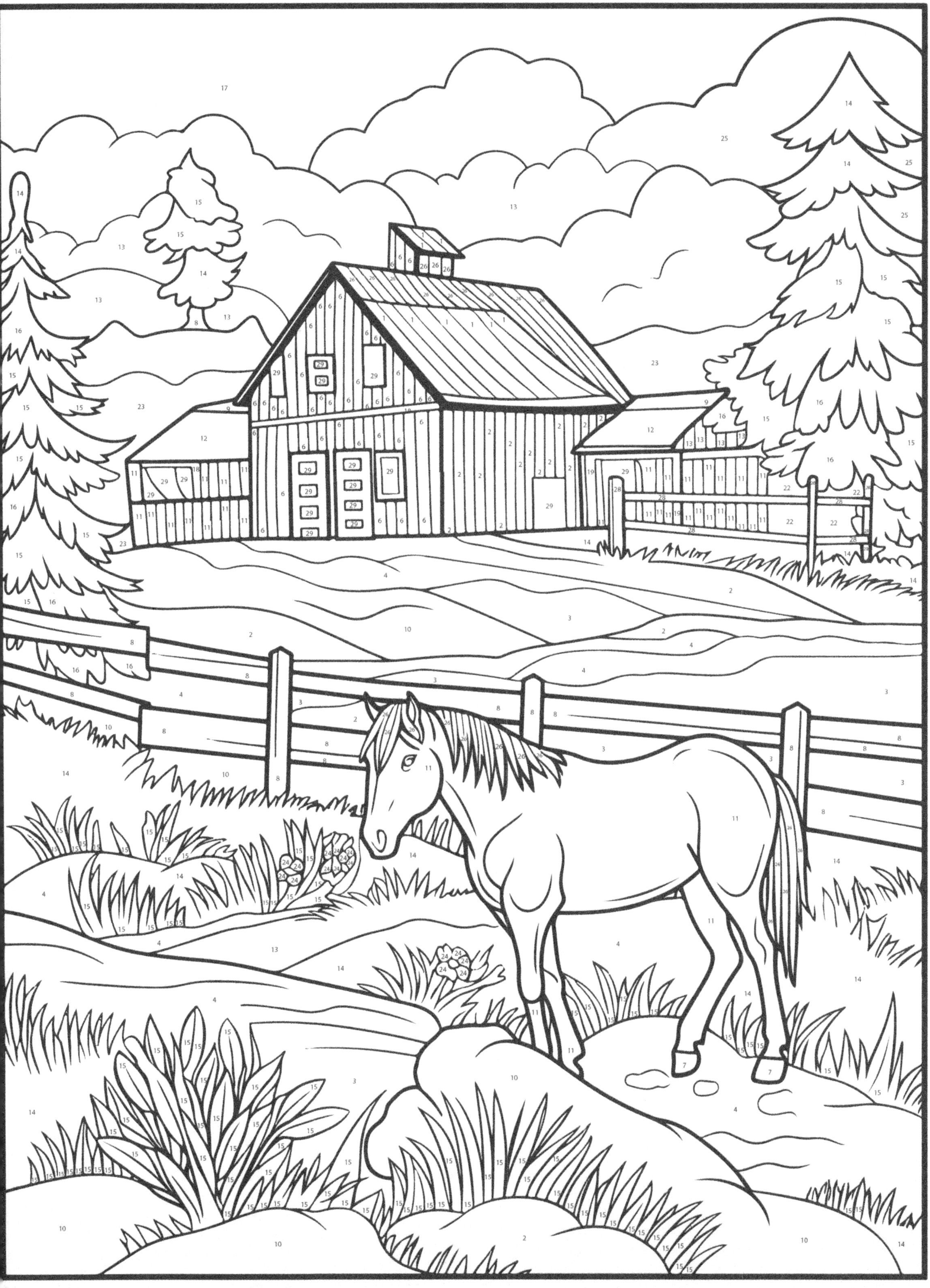

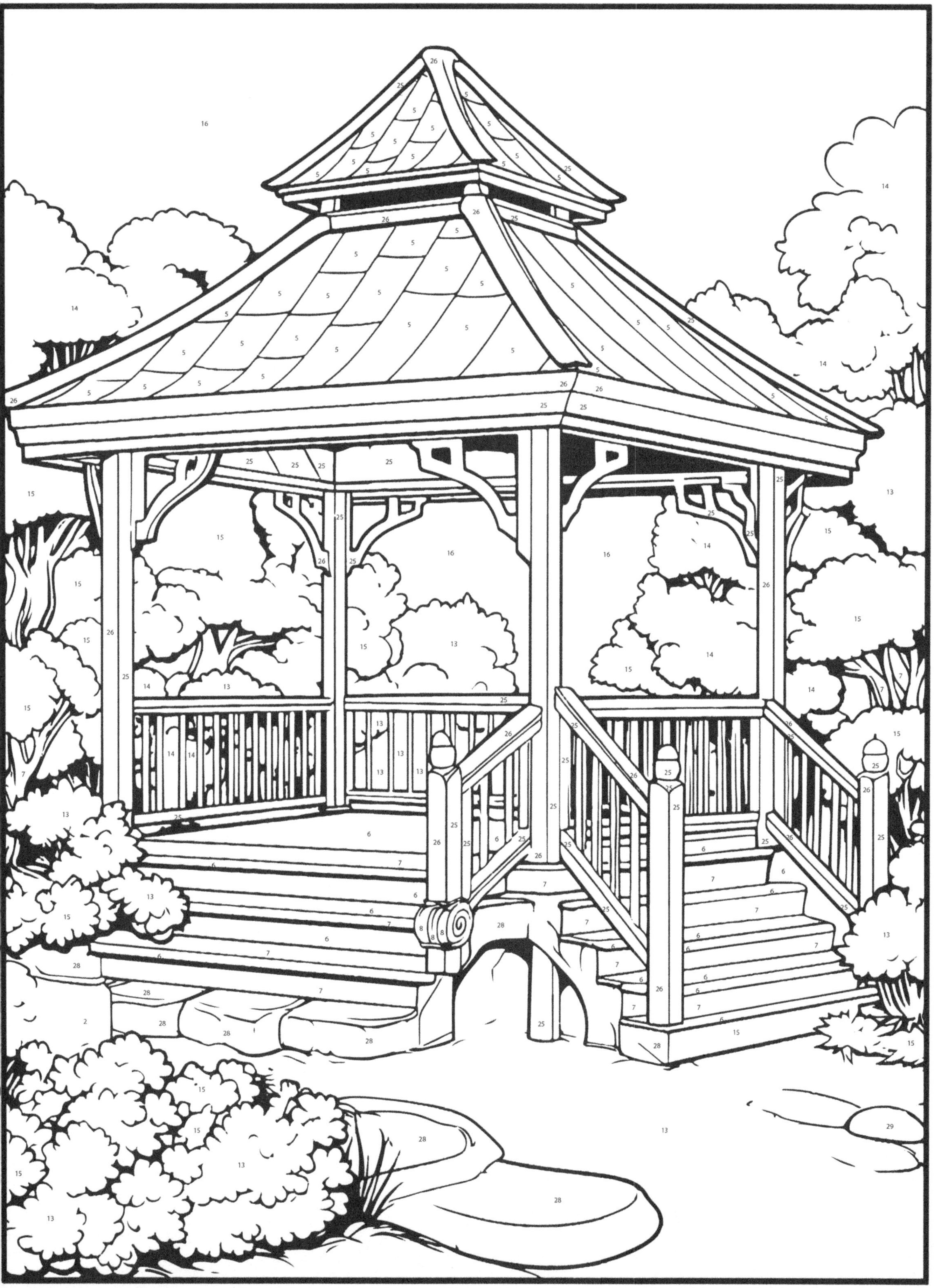

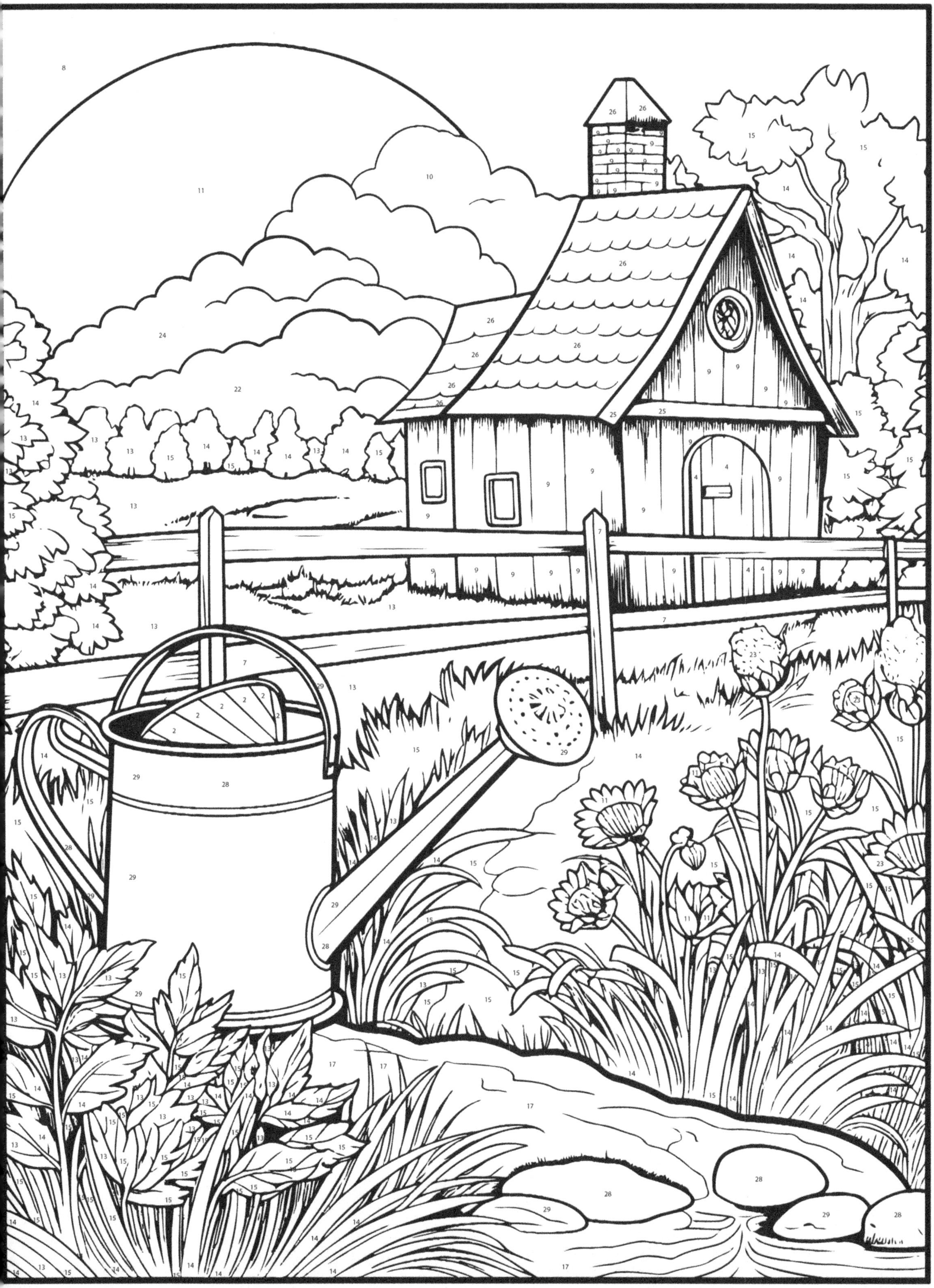

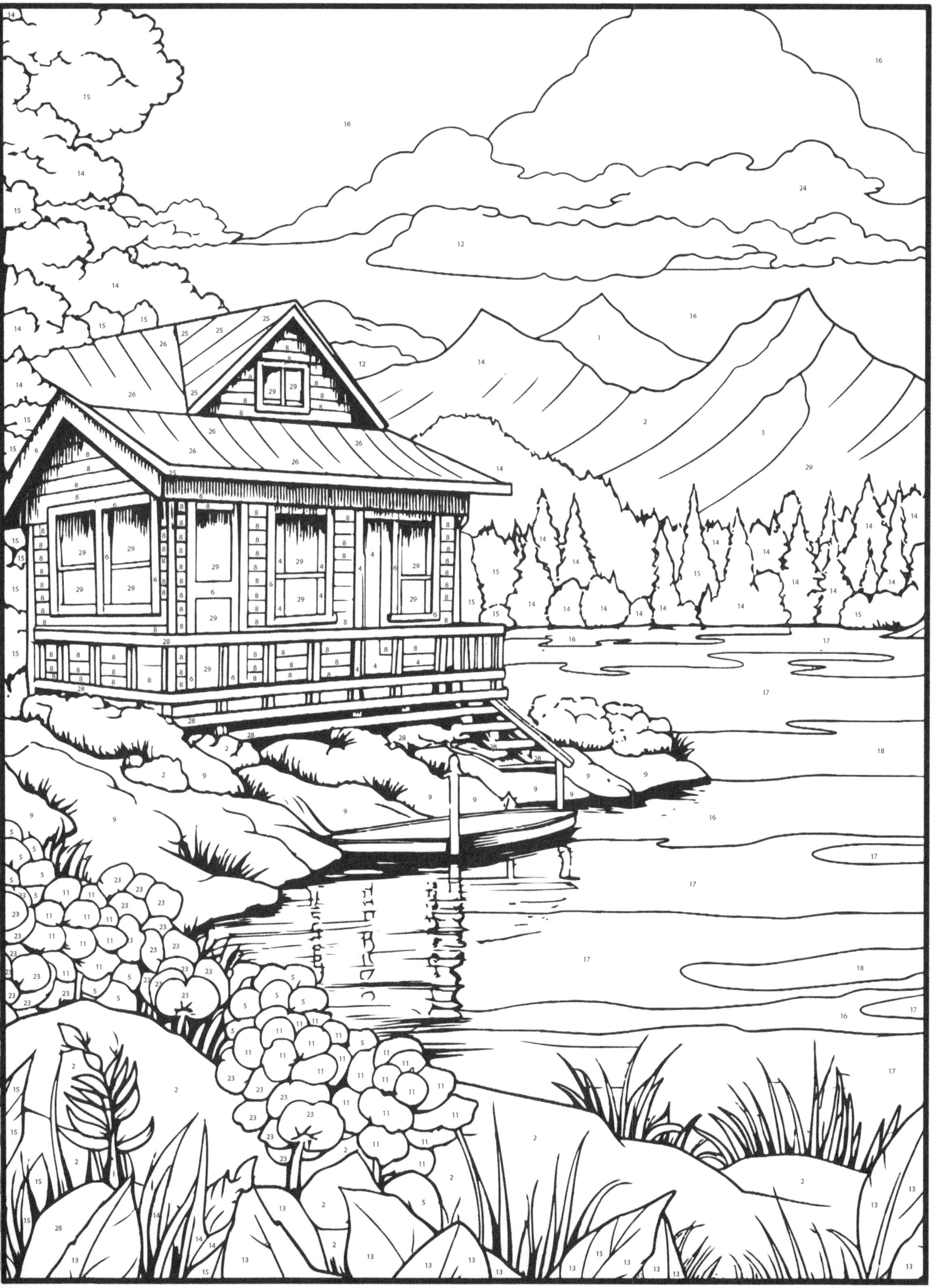

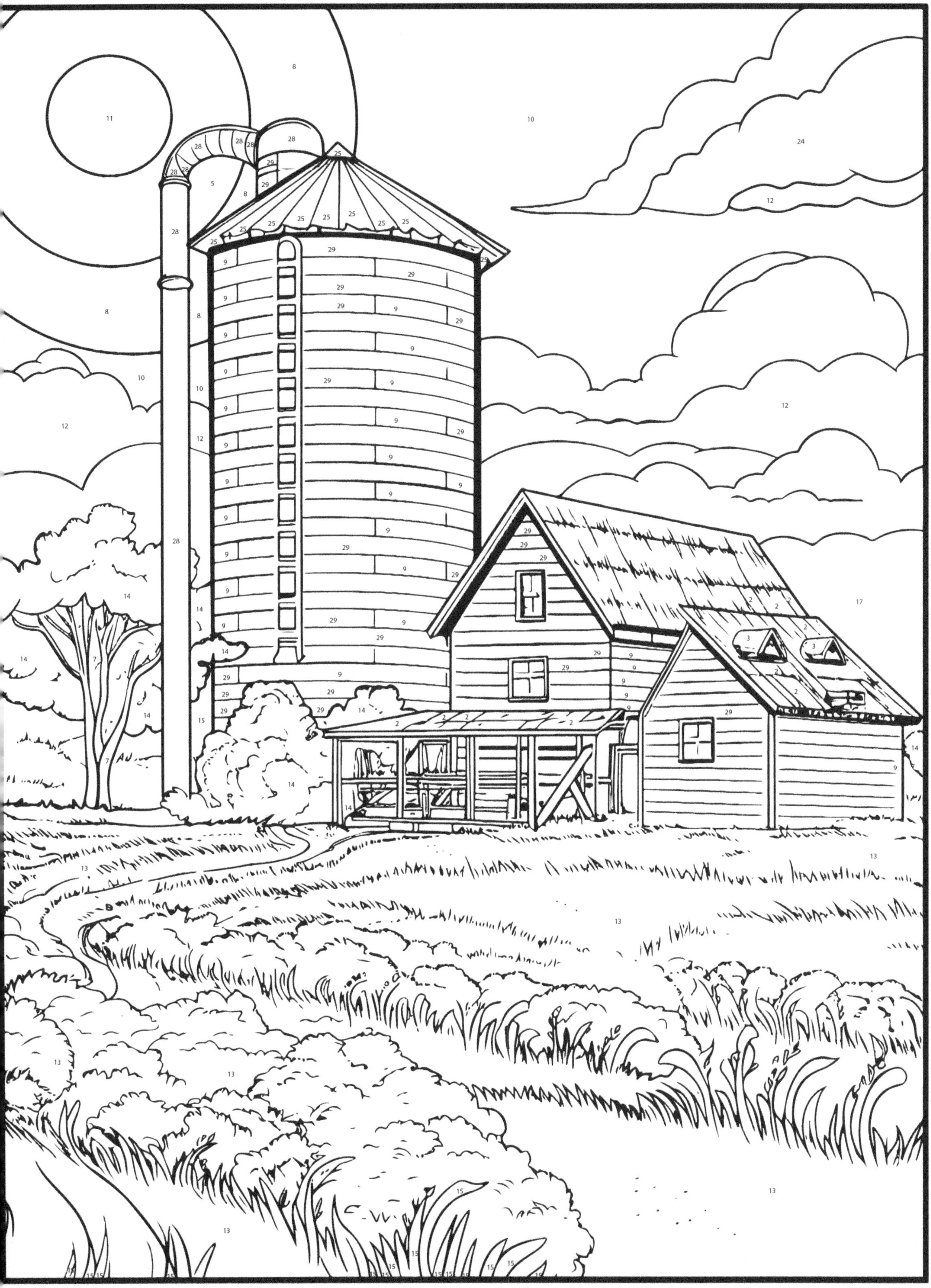

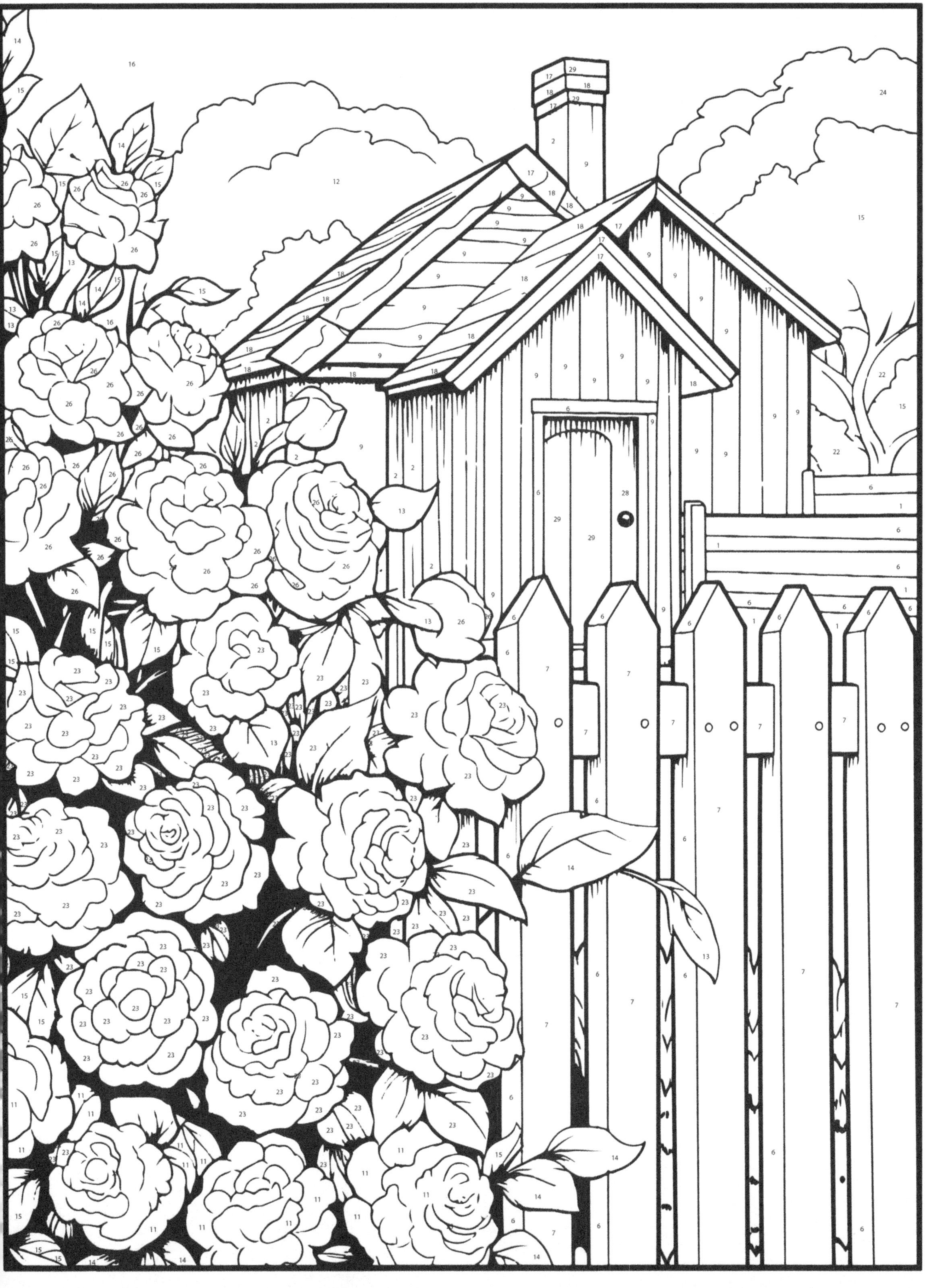

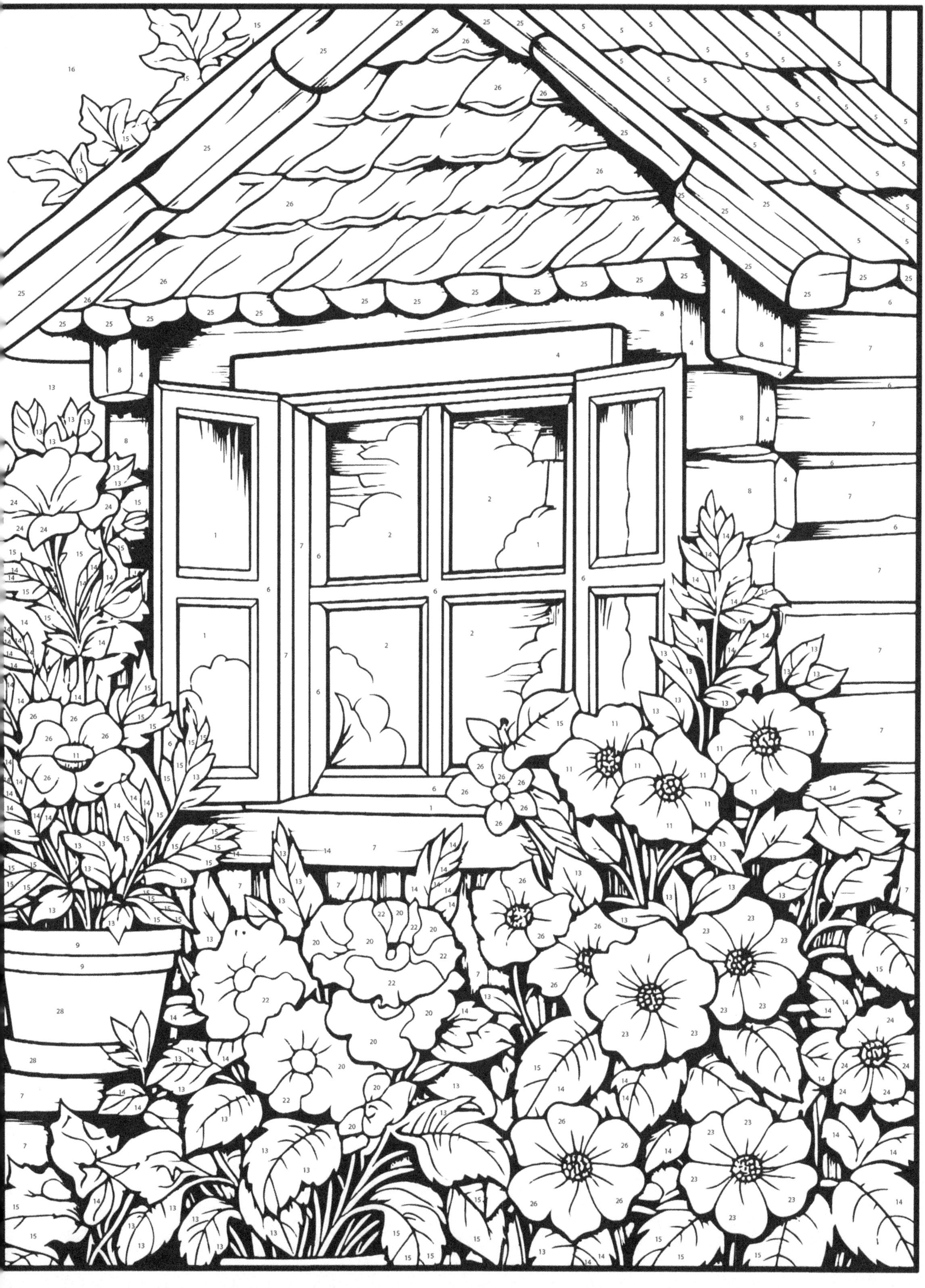

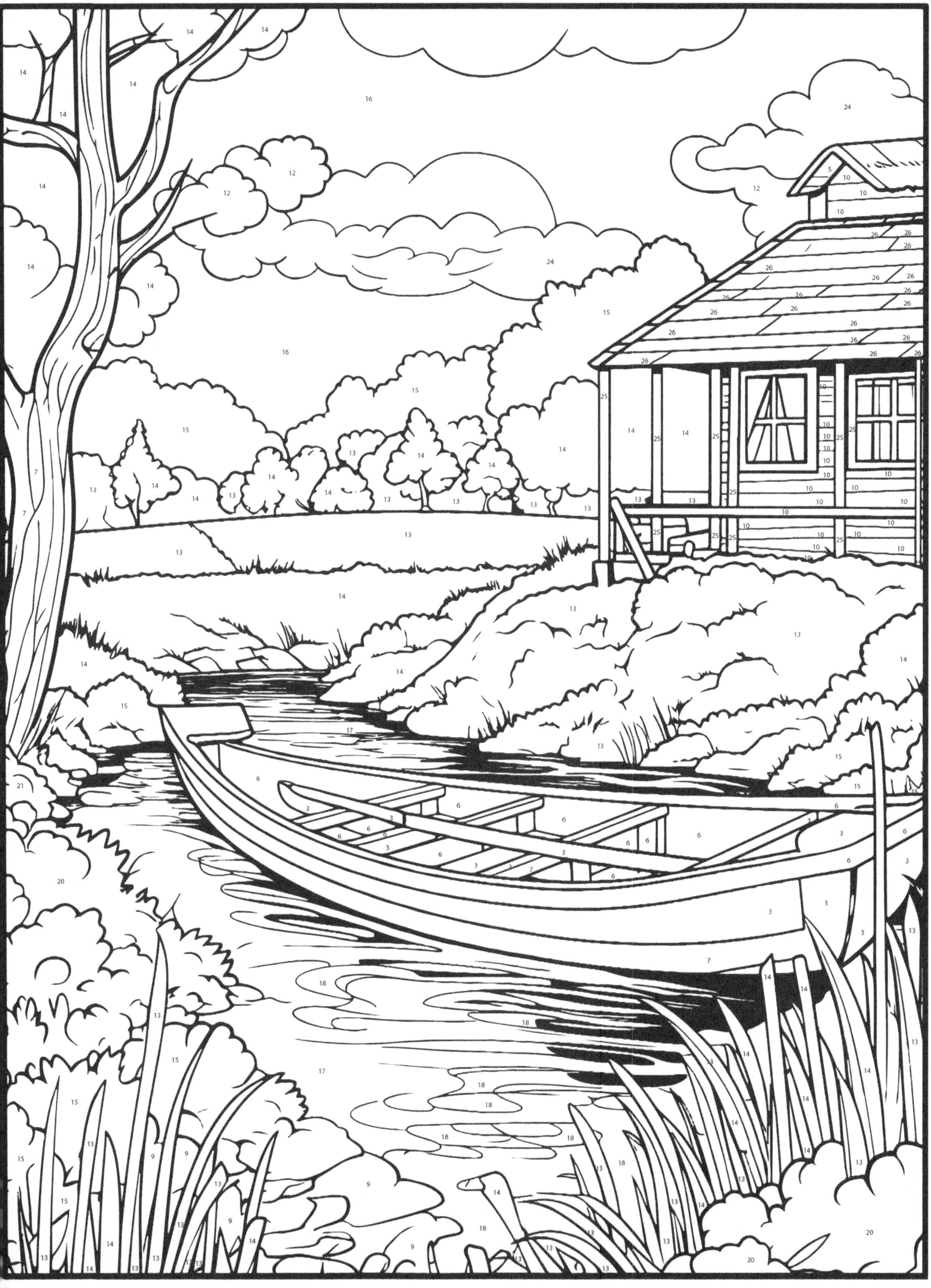

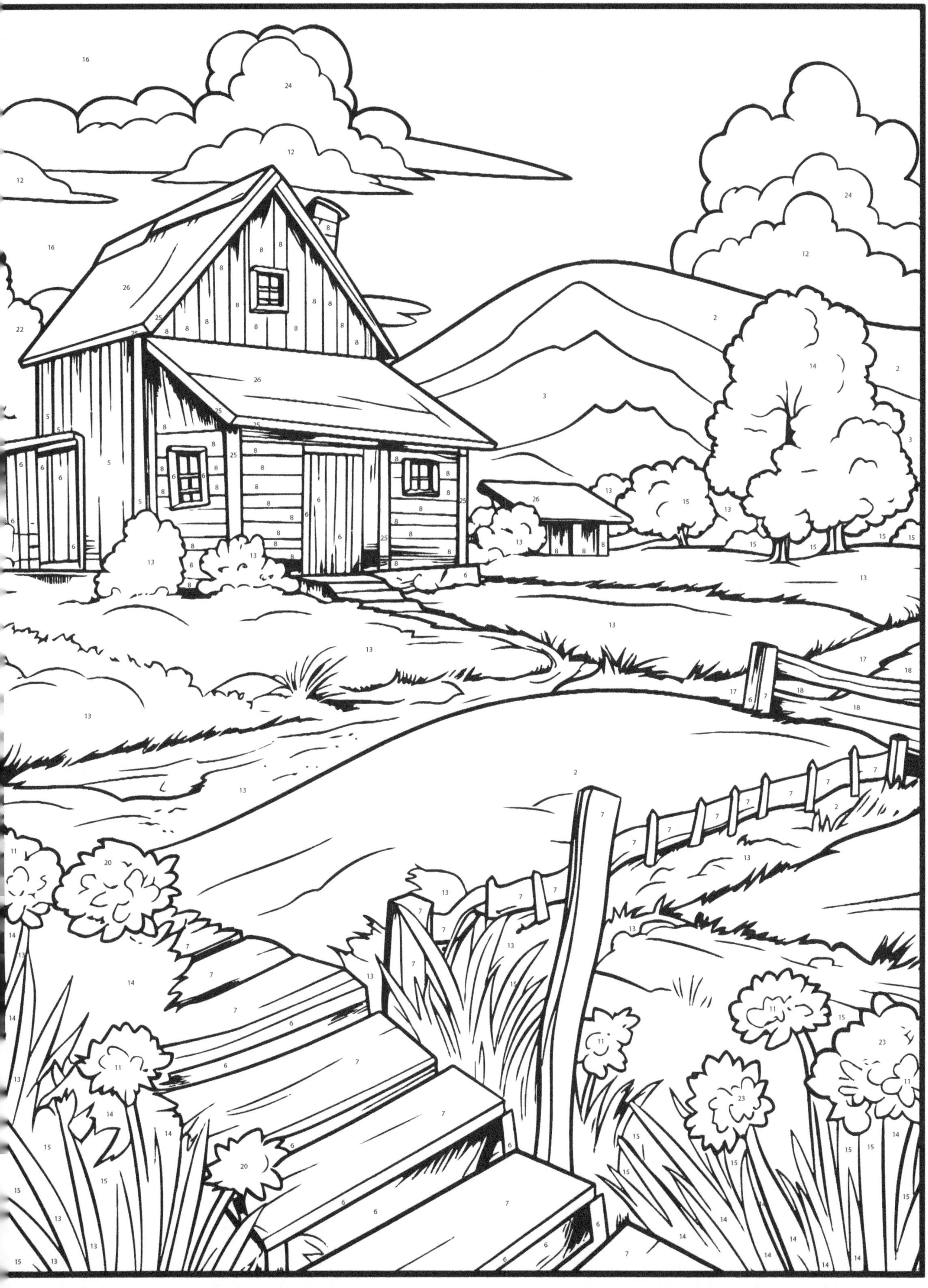

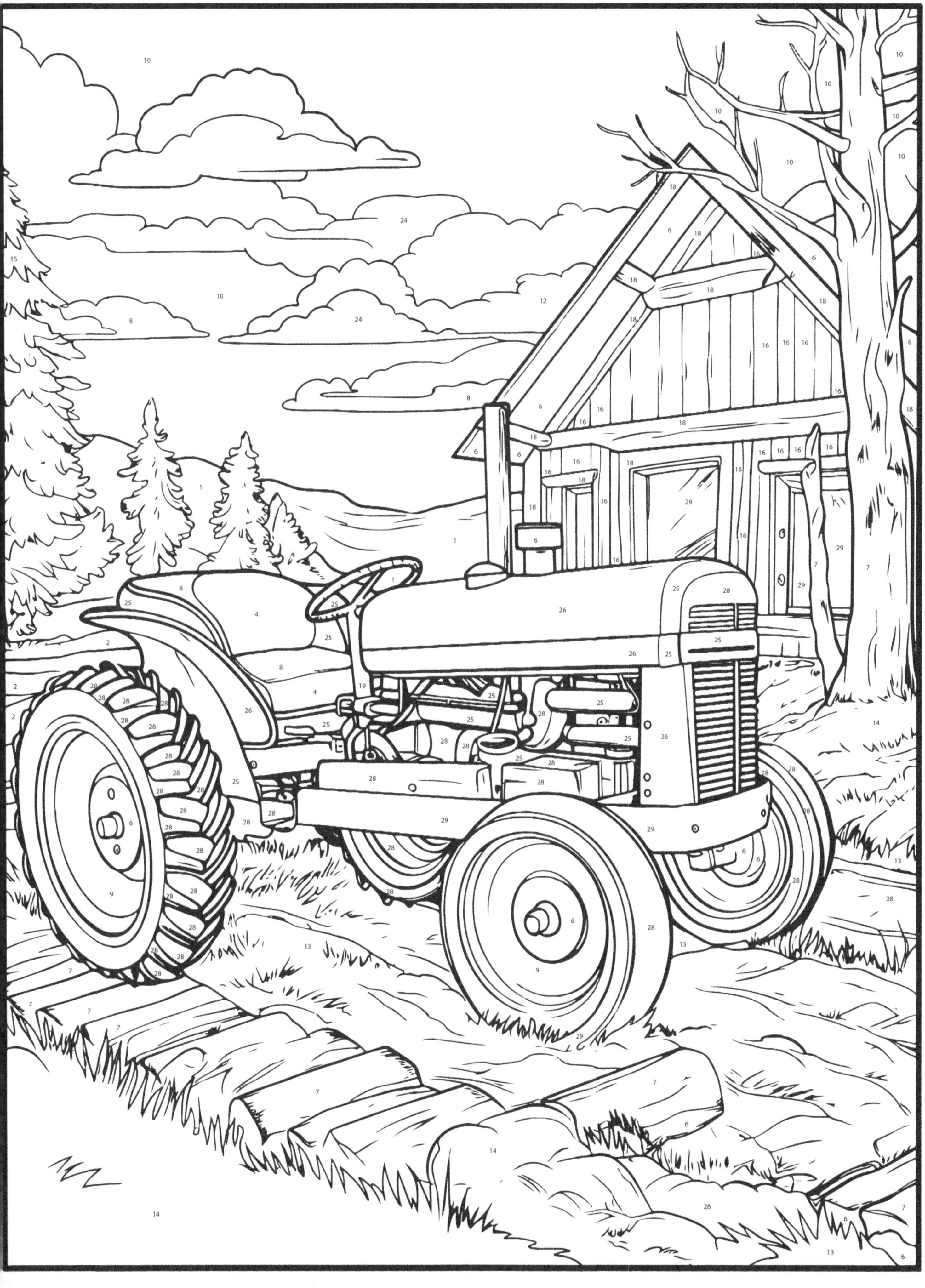

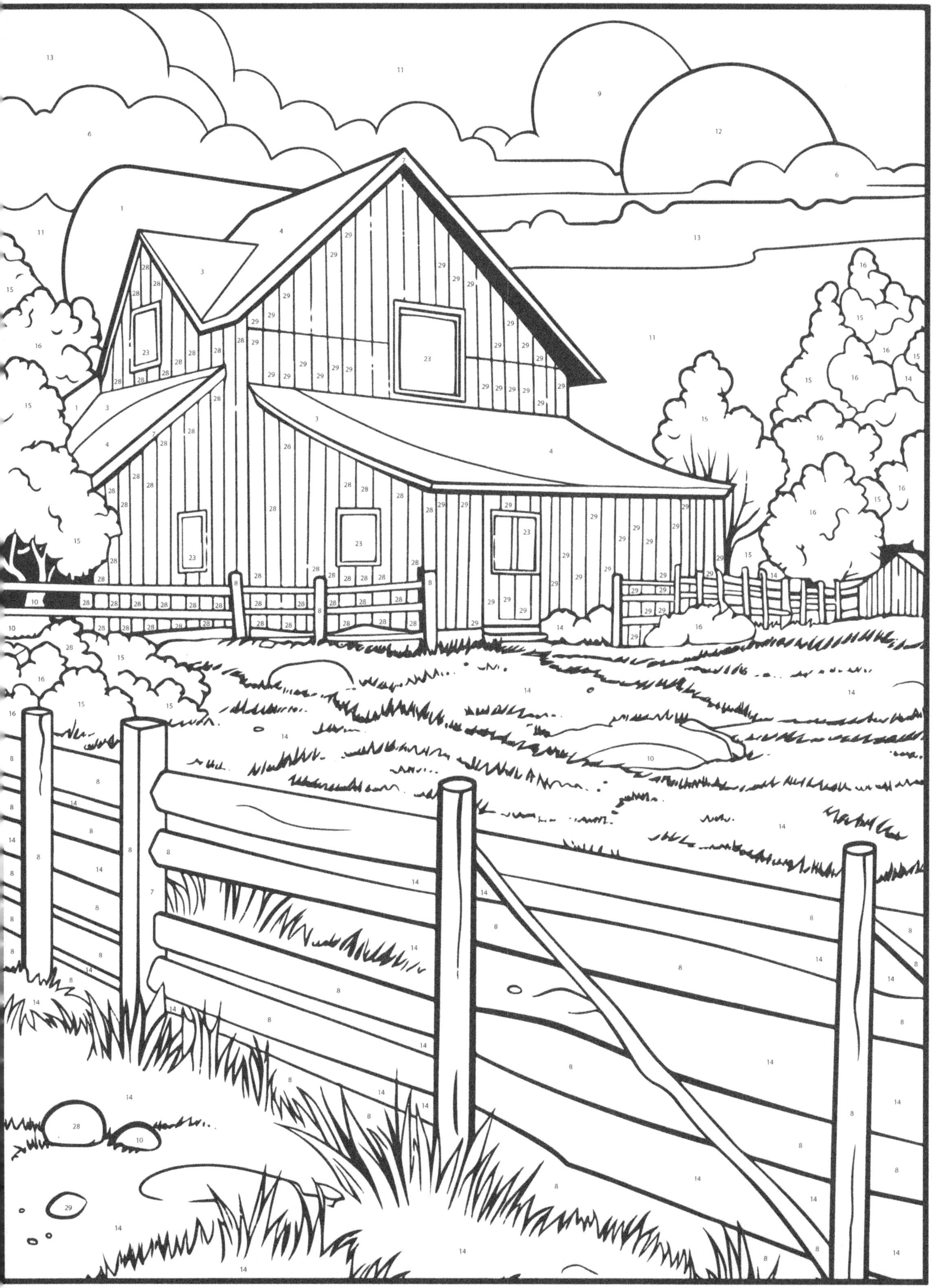

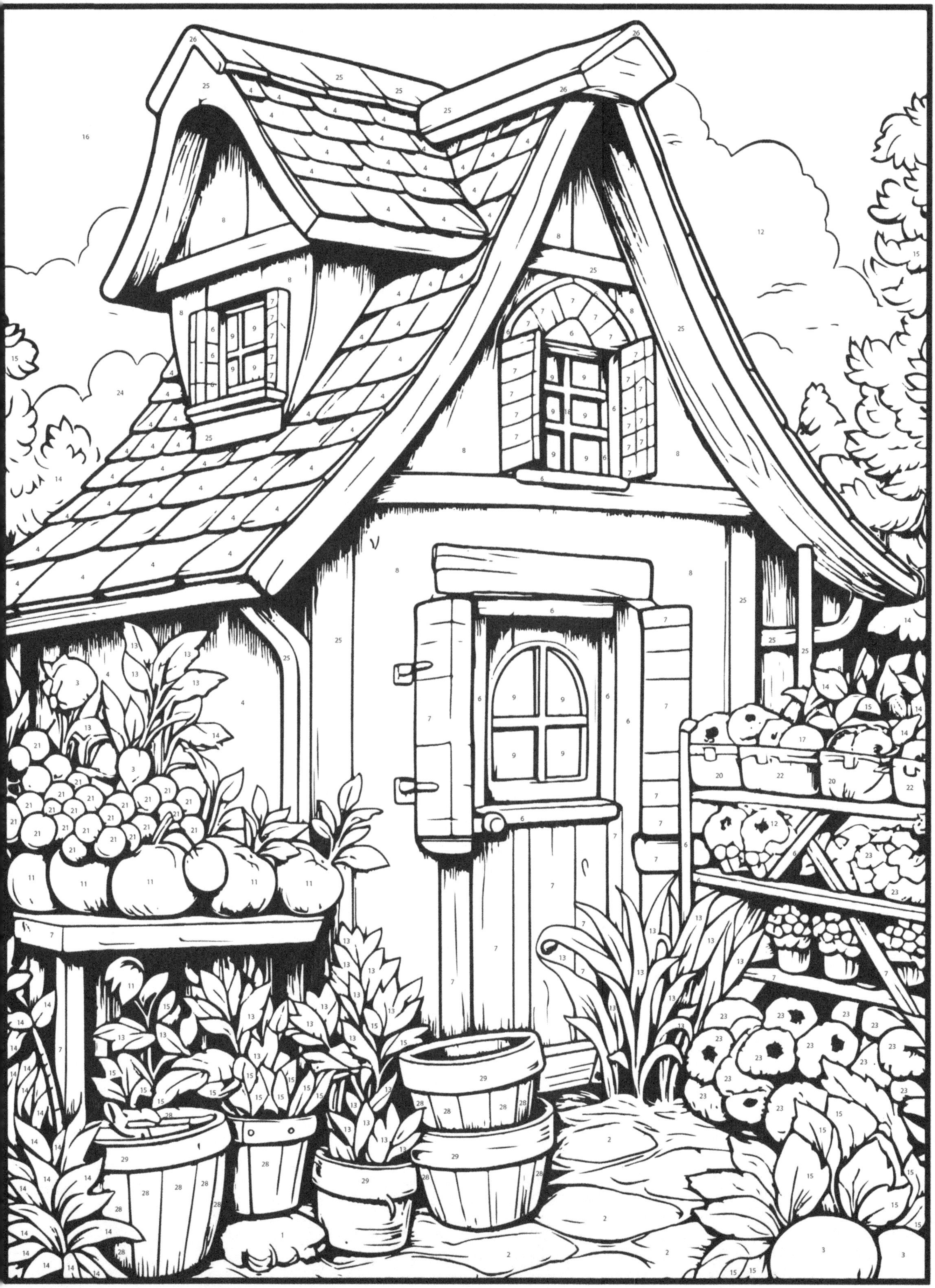

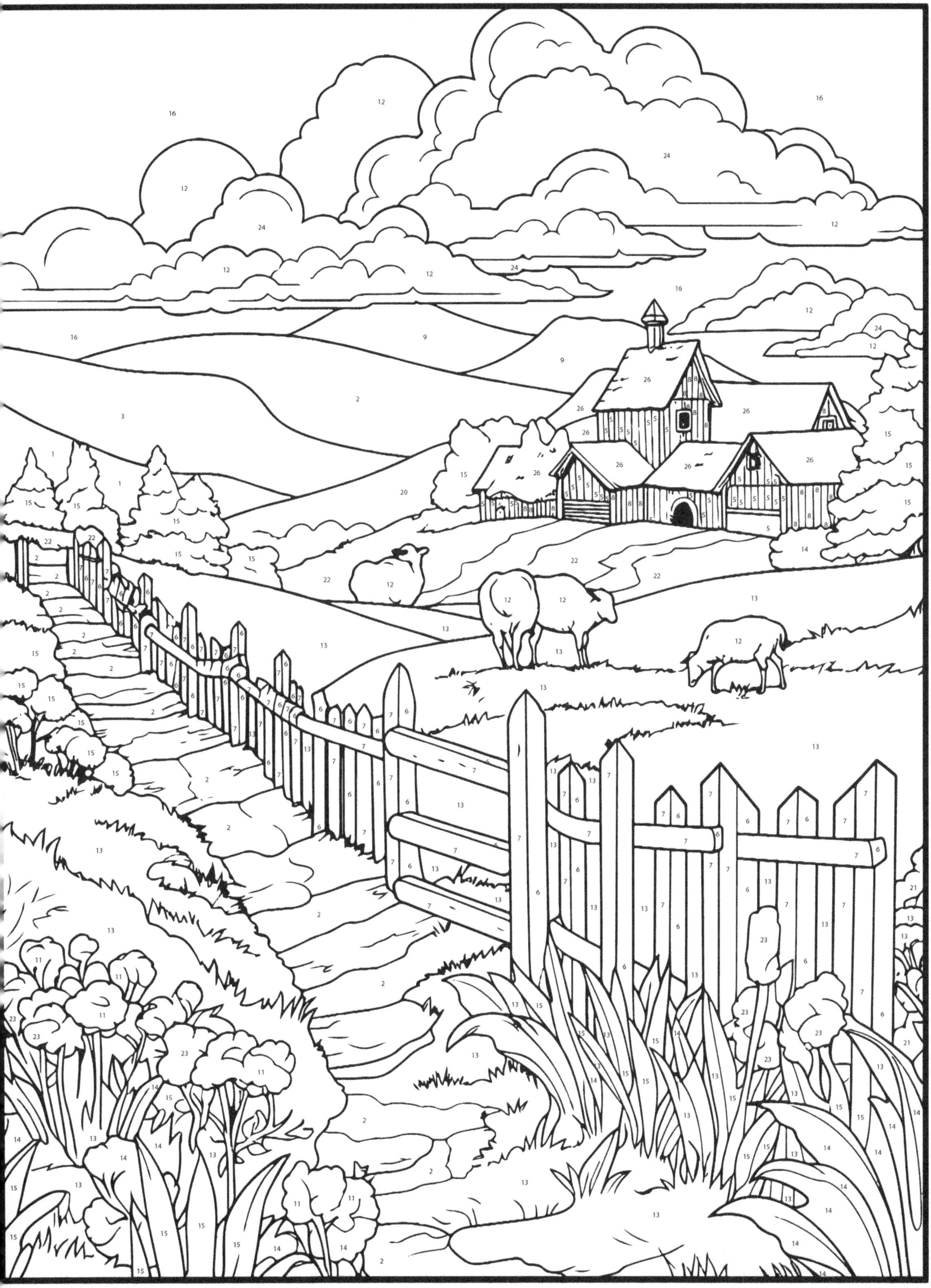

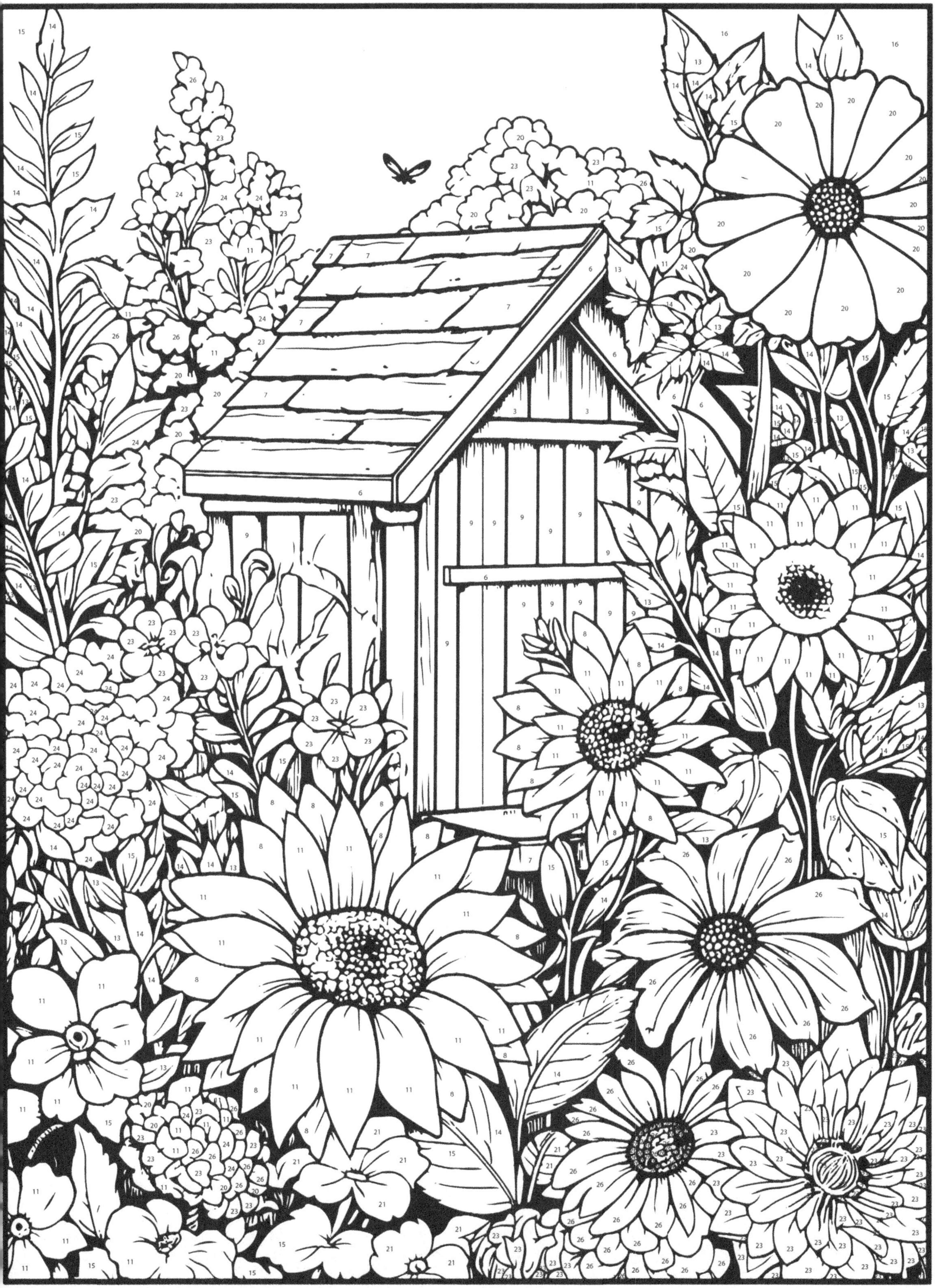

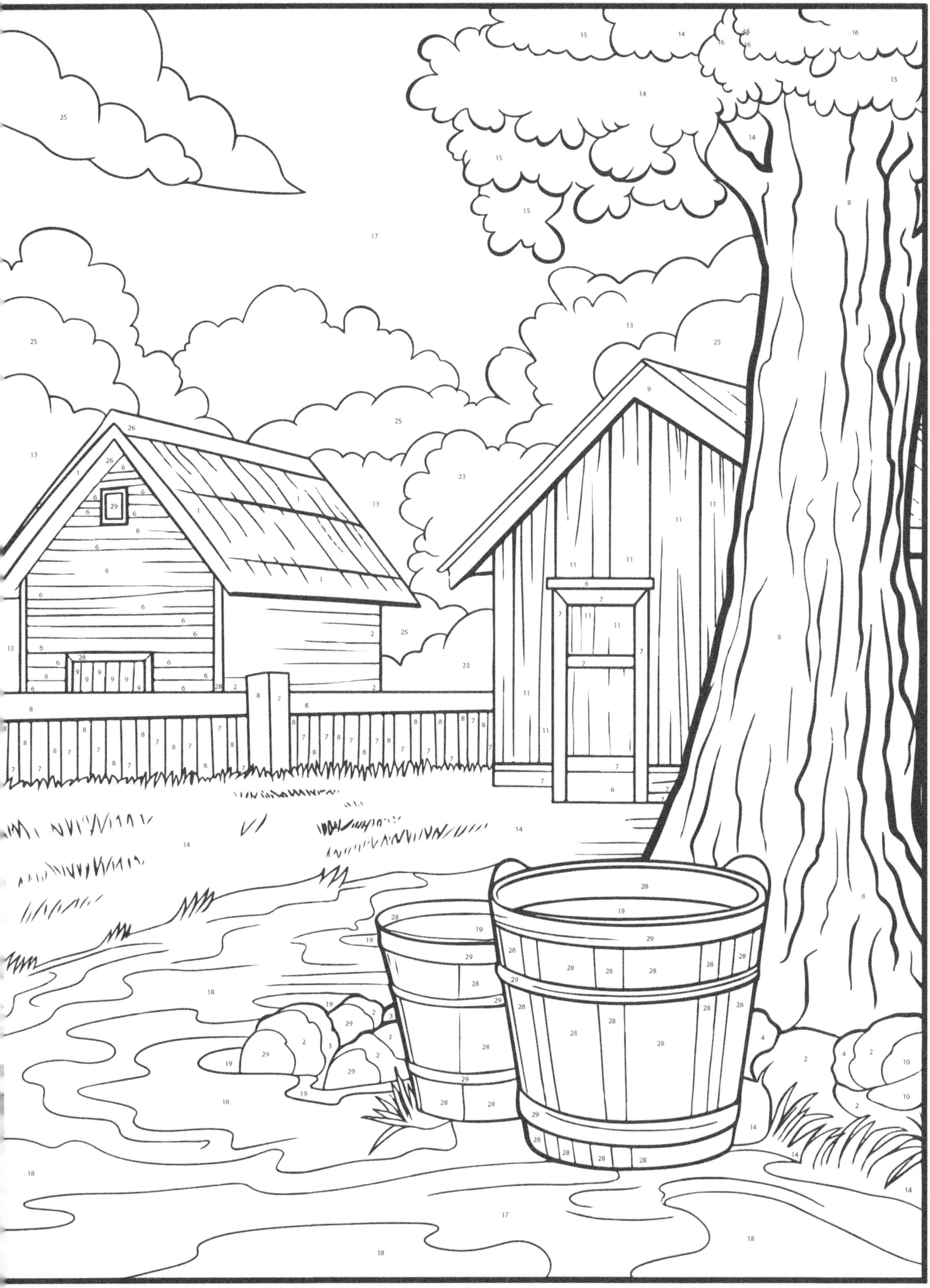

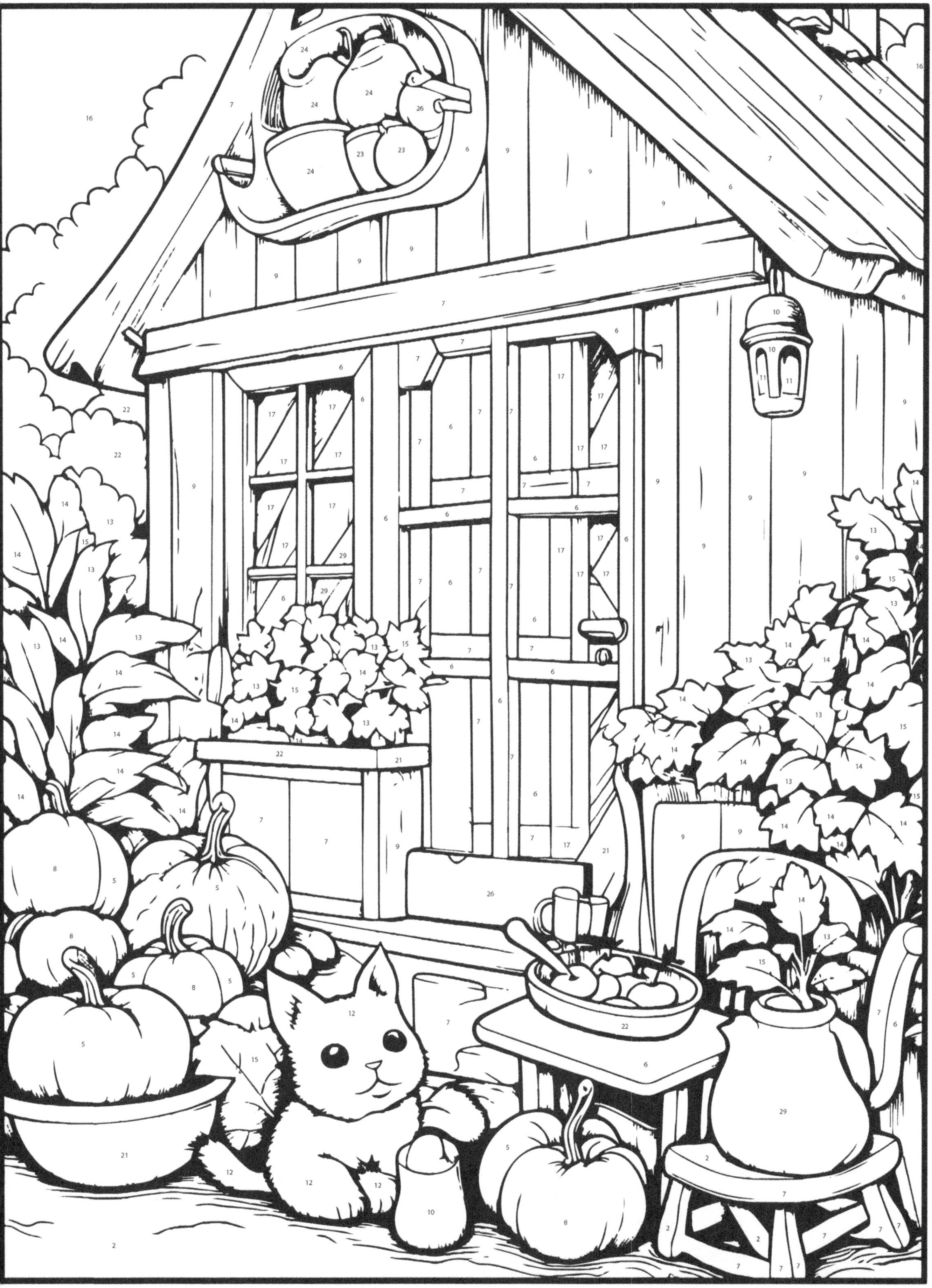

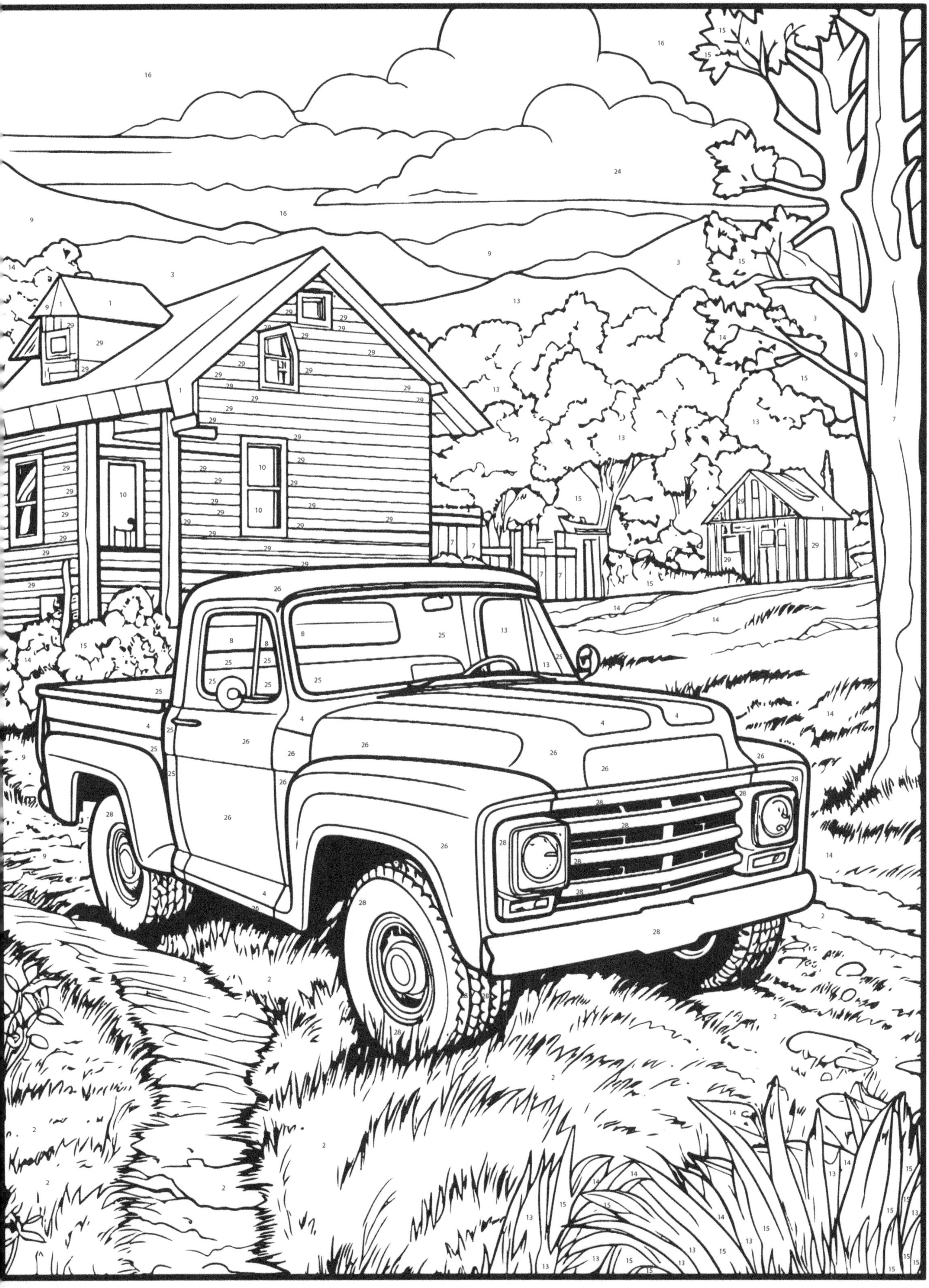

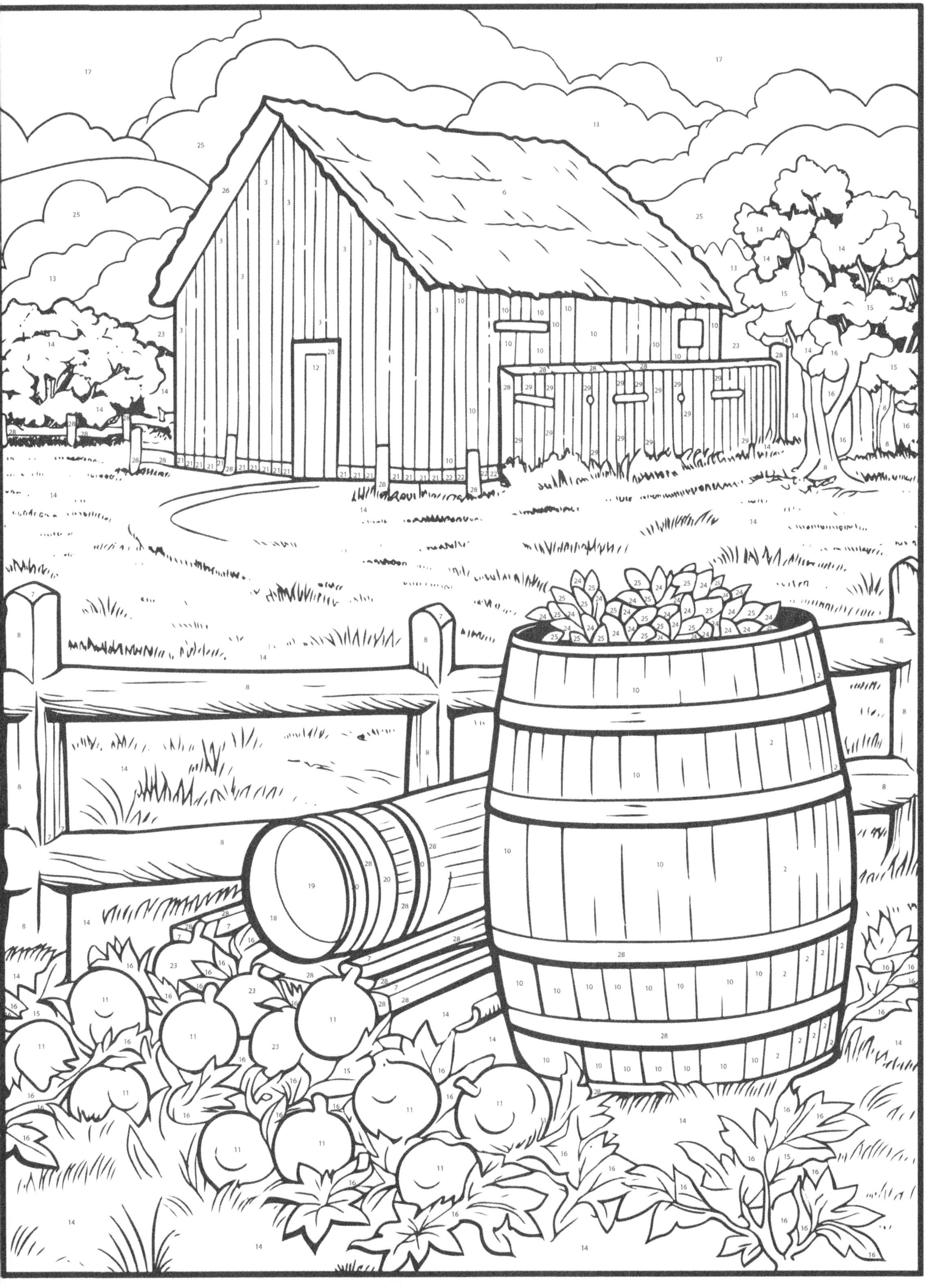

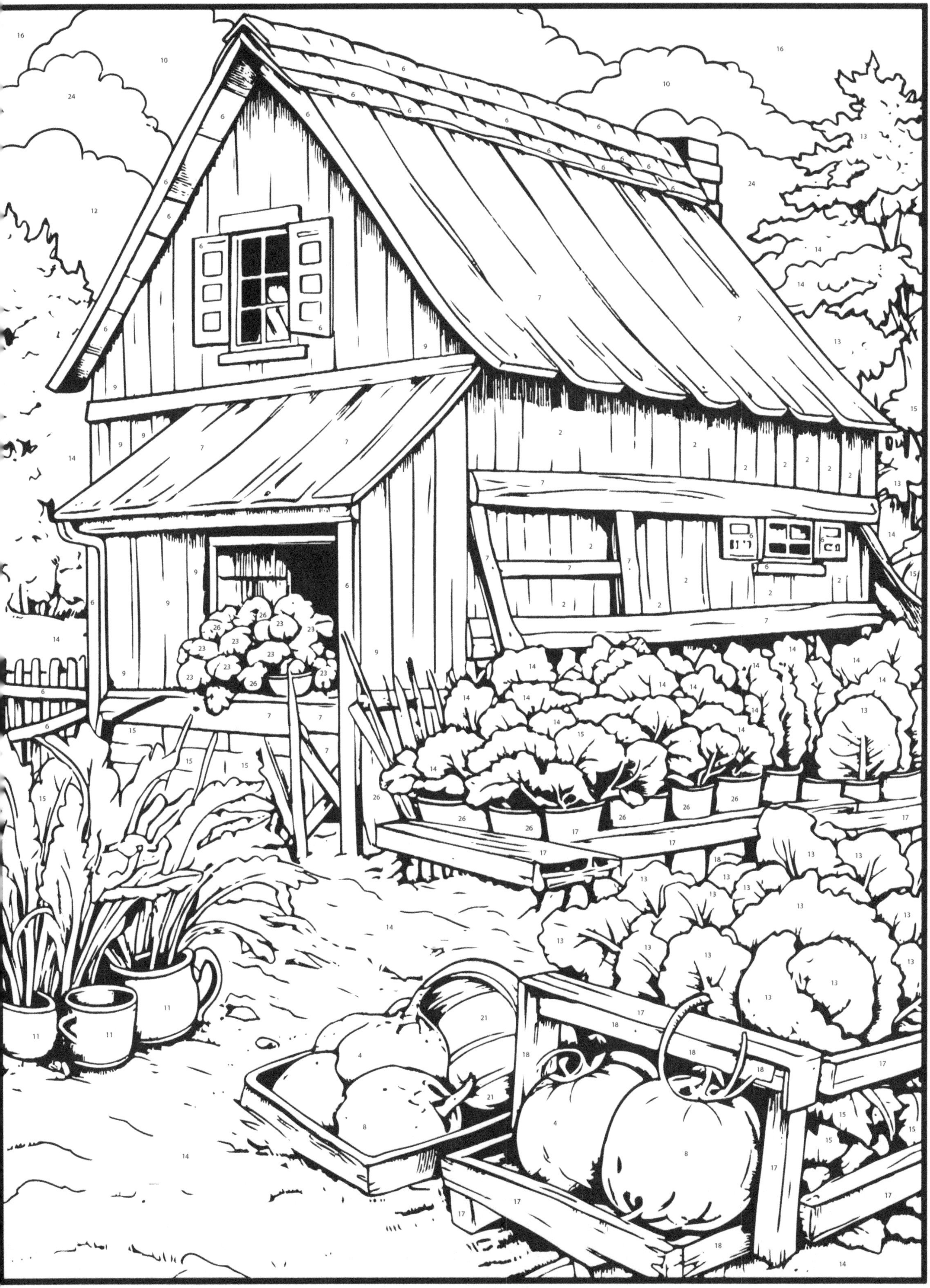

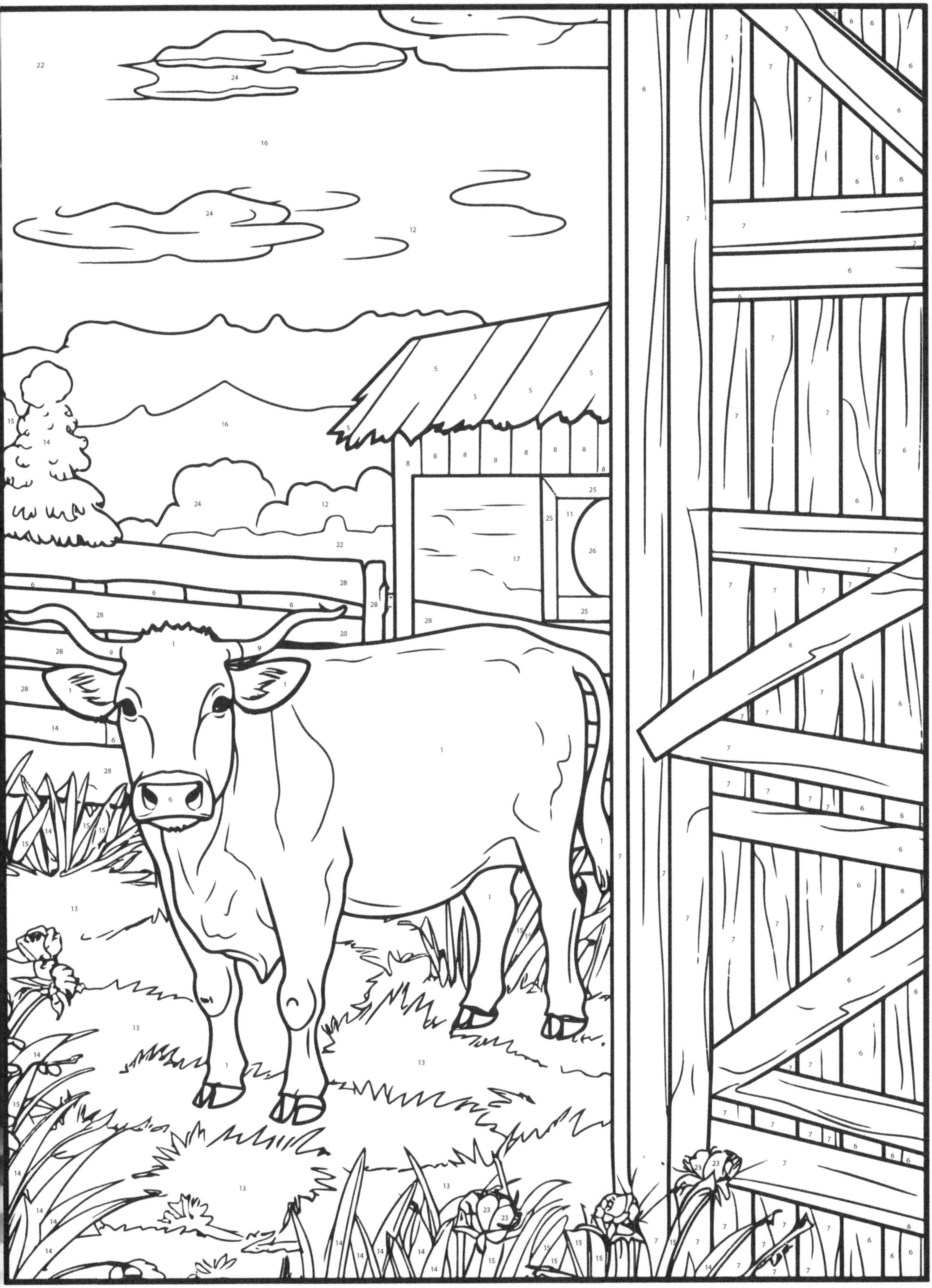

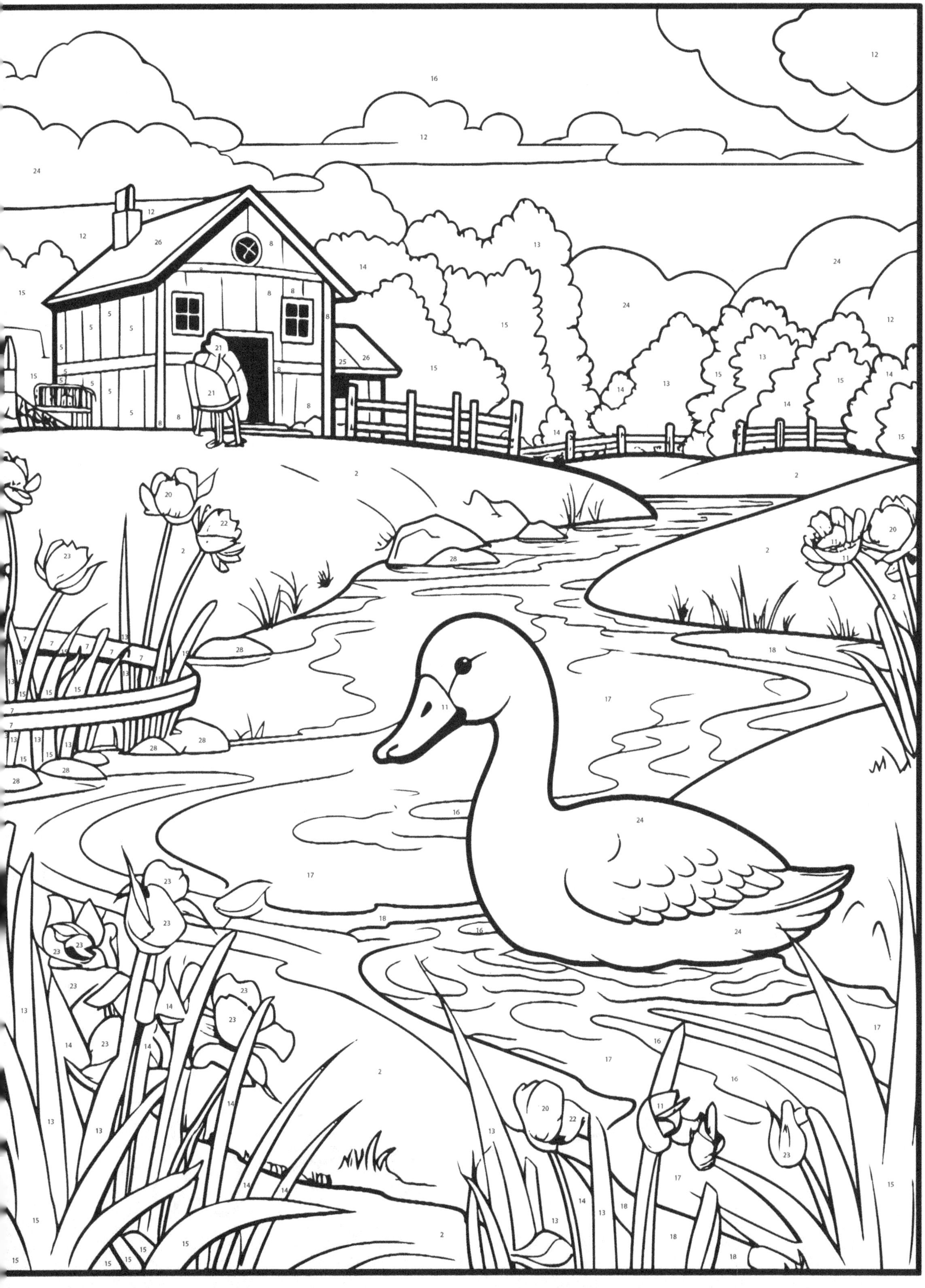

WRITE OUT YOUR
FAVORITE ASPECTS OF THIS BOOK

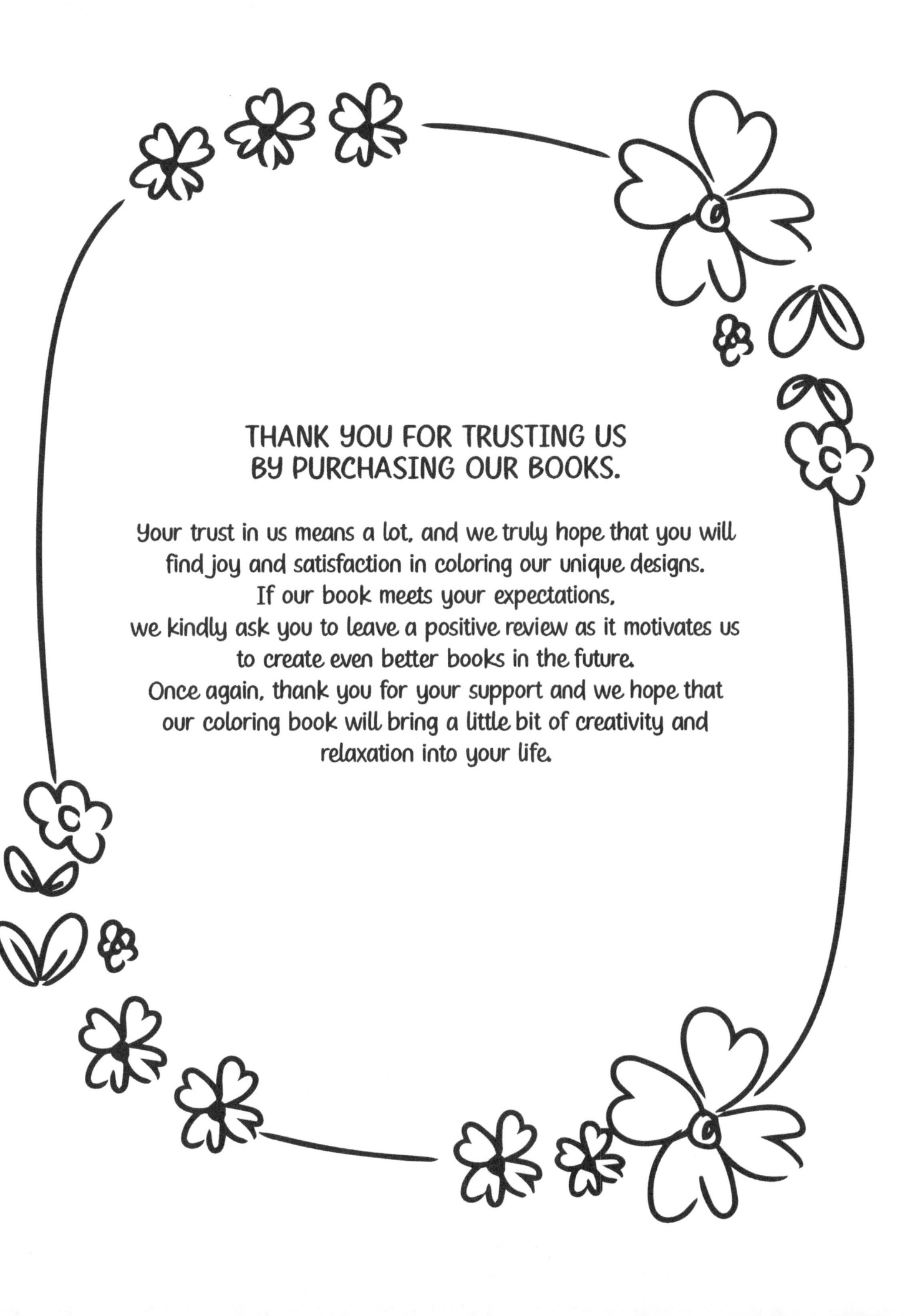

THANK YOU FOR TRUSTING US
BY PURCHASING OUR BOOKS.

Your trust in us means a lot, and we truly hope that you will
find joy and satisfaction in coloring our unique designs.
If our book meets your expectations,
we kindly ask you to leave a positive review as it motivates us
to create even better books in the future.
Once again, thank you for your support and we hope that
our coloring book will bring a little bit of creativity and
relaxation into your life.

Made in the USA
Las Vegas, NV
23 June 2024